Pattern Explorer products available in print or eBook form.

Beginning • Level 1 • Level 2

Written by

Darin Beigie

Graphic Design by

Scott Slyter

THE CRITICAL THINKING CO.™

www.CriticalThinking.com

Phone: 800-458-4849 • Fax: 541-756-1758

1991 Sherman Ave., Suite 200 • North Bend • OR 97459

ISBN 978-1-60144-712-8

Printed in the United States of America by McNaughton & Gunn, Inc., Saline, MI (Sept. 2019)

Table of Contents

About the Author

Darin Beigie teaches mathematics at Harvard-Westlake School in Los Angeles, CA. He develops curriculum and classroom materials to foster greater critical thinking and creativity amongst his students. He publishes frequently in education and teaching journals. He is the author of other books by The Critical Thinking Co.™, including the award-winning *Mathematical Reasoning™ Middle School Supplement* (Grades 7-9), *Math Analogies* Level 3 (Grades 6-7) and Level 4 (Grades 8-9), *Dare to Compare Math* Level 1 (Grades 4-5) and Level 2 (Grades 6-7), *Pattern Explorer* Level 1 (Grades 5-7) and Level 2 (Grades 7-9), and *Critical Thinking Detective™ – Math* (Grades 6-12+). Darin began his career with a Ph.D. in Theoretical Physics at the California Institute of Technology in Pasadena, CA, followed by a Research and Teaching Fellowship at Cornell University's Center for Applied Mathematics in Ithaca, NY. Darin's volunteer work at public middle schools inspired him to become a school teacher, and he has since taught middle school mathematics in New York, Massachusetts, and California.

Introduction

Mathematics and science can be thought of as a search for patterns and structure. Discovery and insight comes when patterns are recognized and structure is understood. From a developmental perspective, the ability to recognize a pattern signals the transition from concrete to abstract thinking. So having children explore pattern problems helps sensitize them to the discovery process that provides a foundation for authentic learning and abstraction.

The pattern problems in this collection are divided into 5 themes: Pattern Predictor, Equality Explorer, Sequence Sleuth, Number Ninja, and Function Finder. To maximize diversity and variation, these themes appear in rotating order for a total of 40 activity sets (8 sets per theme). The activities are independent and self-contained, but they tend to build on one another and get slightly more sophisticated as the collection progresses. So students are generally encouraged to work on the earlier sets first and build up from there, although they should feel free to pick and choose as well.

The patterns are appropriate for children in Grades 3-4, although their experiences with these activities may vary widely depending upon readiness for abstraction. Younger students may find each activity to be like a small project, worthy of rich exploration and deep thinking. Older students may be equipped to uncover patterns with much greater agility and speed. In all situations, and at whatever pace and facility, the transition from concrete to abstract thinking is worthwhile.

All activities provide space for work to be shown, but students are encouraged to have scratch paper at hand in case uncovering a pattern merits deeper investigation, such as guess-and-check, drawing diagrams, and making lists or charts. Calculators are never needed, and their use is discouraged.

Each activity is accompanied by hints and solutions, in separate sections following the activities. The hints provide occasional nudges to help steer a student in the right direction. The solutions are generally detailed and comprehensive. There are many ways to solve and explain a pattern problem, and the solutions we provide are not intended to be unique. The reader may come up with many other wonderful ways to solve and describe the patterns. The answers, however, are usually unique.

We encourage students to pursue these pattern problems with a sense of adventure and perseverance. Some pattern discoveries may come quickly, while others may require patience and determination. Regardless, the pattern exploration offers rich and authentic experiences in mathematical reasoning.

6. Pattern Predictor 2

1. Look at the pattern and then draw stage 4. For later stages, make a drawing if it helps you answer the questions.

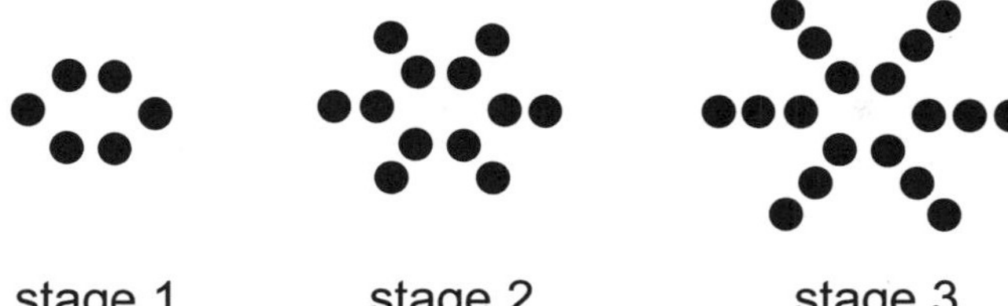

stage 1 stage 2 stage 3 stage 4

2. How many circles are there at stage 4?

3. How many circles are there at stage 5?

4. How many circles are there at stage 6? Complete the table to show the number of circles for stages 1 through 6.

stage	1	2	3	4	5	6
number of circles	6					

5. How many circles are there at stage 7?

6. How many circles are there at stage 10?

7. At what stage will there be 54 circles?

8. At what stage will there be 78 circles?

6. Pattern Predictor 2 (continued)

9. Look at the pattern and then draw stage 5. For later stages, make a drawing if it helps you answer the questions.

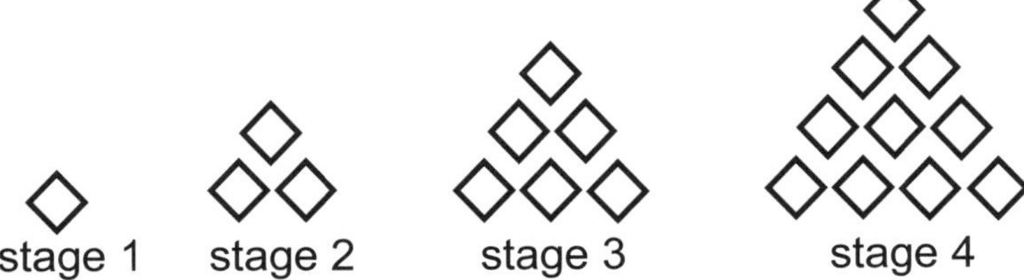

stage 5

10. How many diamonds are there at stage 5?

11. How many diamonds are there at stage 6?

12. Determine how many diamonds there are at stage 7 and stage 8 and then complete the table summarizing your results.

stage	number of diamonds
1	1
2	3
3	
4	
5	
6	
7	
8	

13. Explain in words the pattern you see in the table. Then state the number of diamonds in stage 9 and stage 10.

- stage 9: ______
- stage 10: ______

7. Equality Explorer 2

Each 2D shape represents a different whole number. Use the equations to find their value.

1.

♥ − 5 = 11

♥ + ⬠ + ⬠ = 30

⬠ = ___ ♥ = ___

2.

☁ − ⏢ = 5

☁ + ☁ = 26

☁ = ___ ⏢ = ___

3.

☾ + ☾ + ☾ = ★

★ + ★ − 4 = 20

★ = ___ ☾ = ___

4.

✡ + ✡ − ☺ = 14

☺ + ☺ − 3 = 9

✡ = ___ ☺ = ___

5.

20 − △ = 11

ϟ + ϟ + △ = 19

▱ − ϟ = 6

△ = ___ ϟ = ___ ▱ = ___

6.

◆ − ✦ = 5

✦ − □ = 14

□ + □ + 8 = 10

□ = ___ ◆ = ___ ✦ = ___

8. Sequence Sleuth 2

Fill in all the blanks for the sequences.

	1st	2nd	3rd	4th	5th	6th	7th	8th	9th	10th	11th	12th
1.	7	11	15	19	23					43		
2.	98	92	86	80	74							32
3.	0	15		45		75	90				150	
4.	2	15	28		54			93		119		
5.	149	140	131		113	104			77			

Create a sequence of numbers to answer the word problems.

6. On Monday Jamie has 14 quarters in his piggy bank. On Tuesday he has 17 quarters in his piggy bank. On Wednesday he has 20 quarters in his piggy bank. If the pattern continues, how many quarters will Jamie have in his piggy bank on Tuesday of next week?

7. Laura is selling chocolate bars to raise money for charity. On Monday she has 76 bars left to sell. On Tuesday she has 72 bars left to sell. On Wednesday she has 68 bars left to sell. If the pattern continues, how many chocolate bars will Laura have left to sell on Thursday of next week?

9. Number Ninja 2

Find the pattern and fill in the missing number in the middle circle. The first one is done as an example.

1.

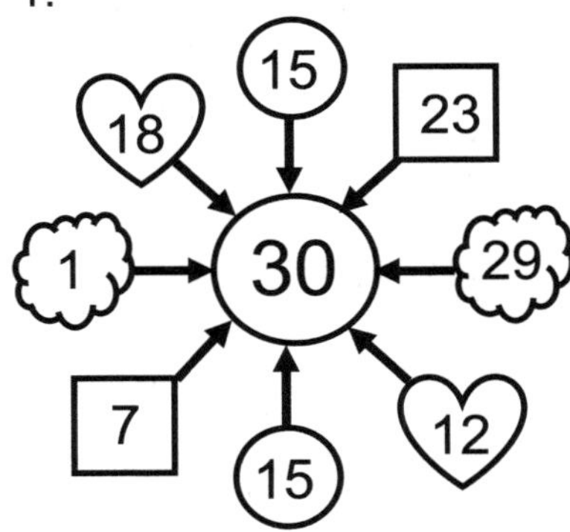

2.

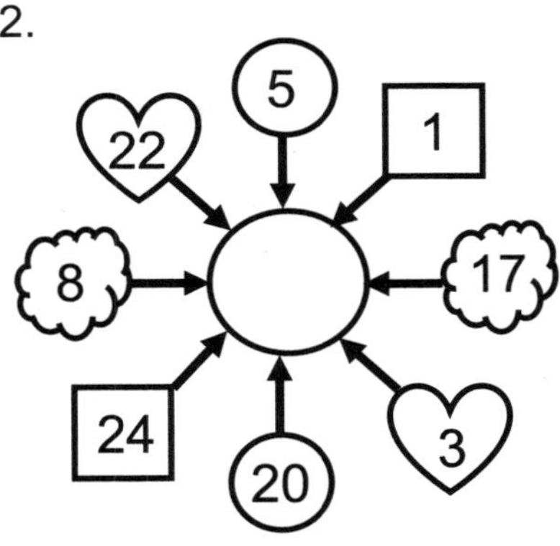

3.

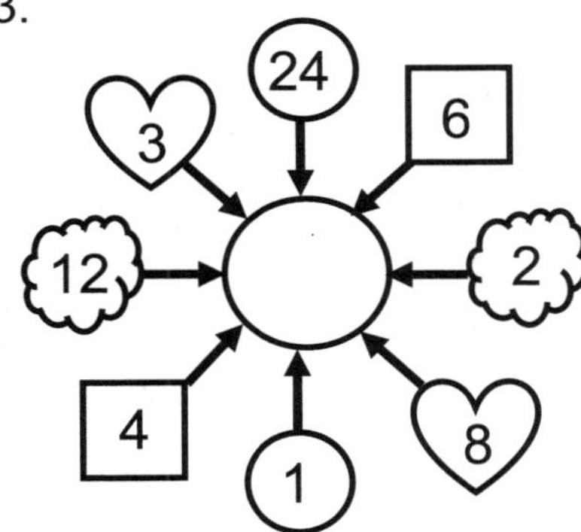

4.

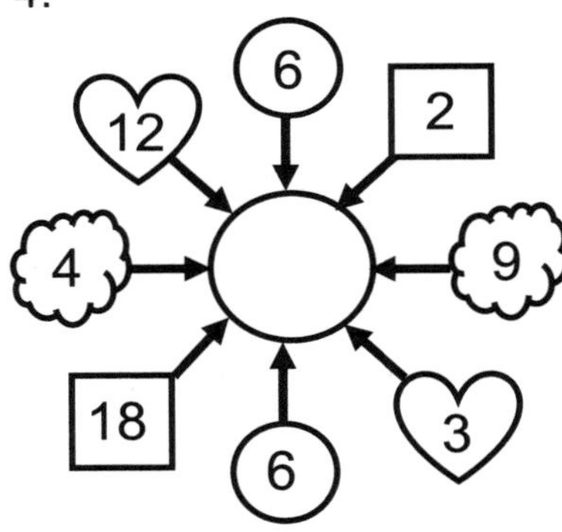

5.

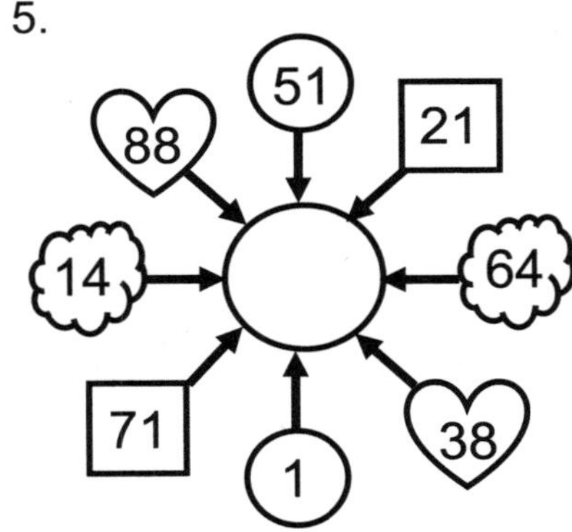

6.

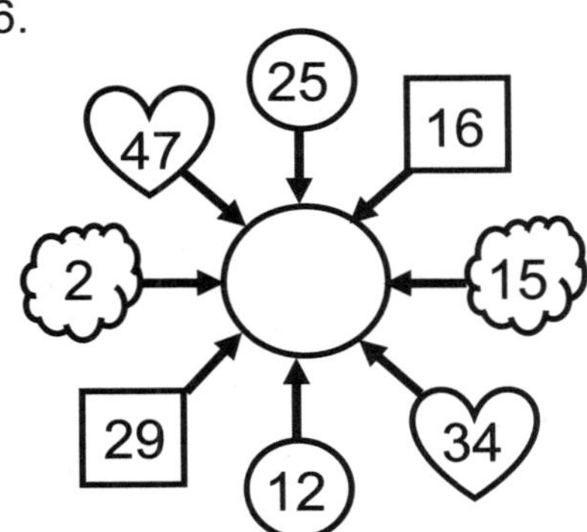

7.

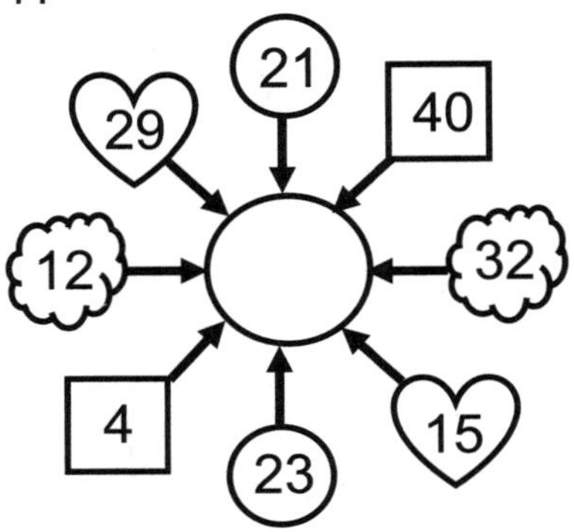

8.

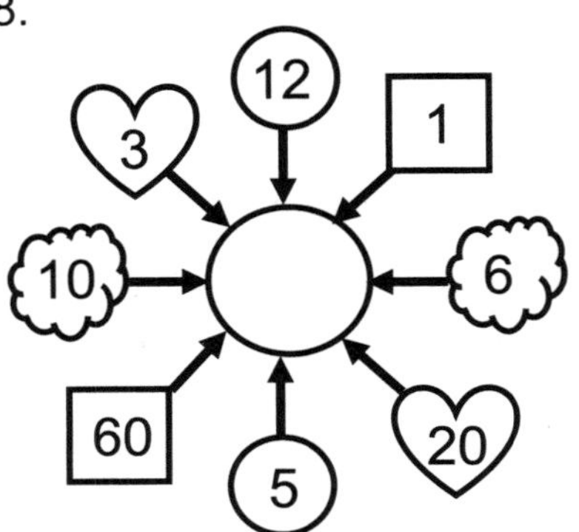

9.

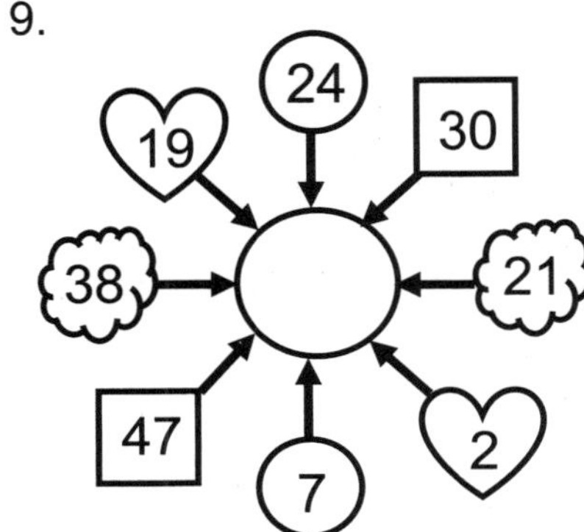

10. Function Finder 2

Each question gives 5 examples of 4 numbers related by a secret pattern. Discover the pattern and then fill in the missing numbers.

1. Examples:

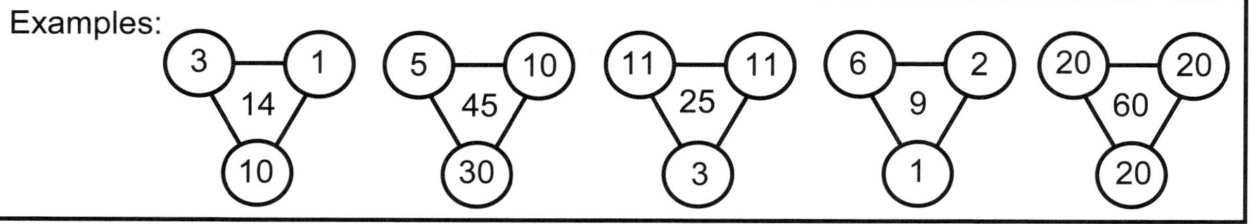

a. b.

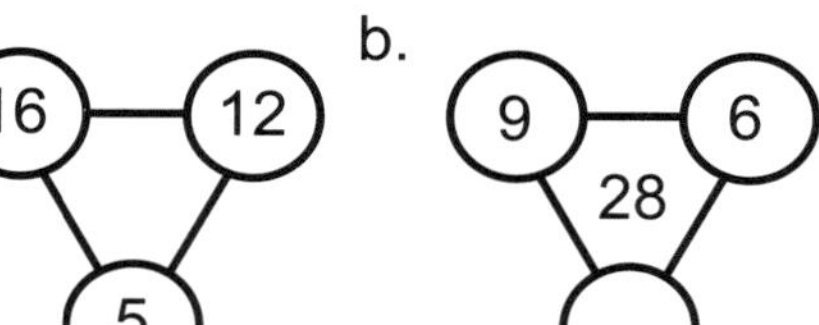

c. d.

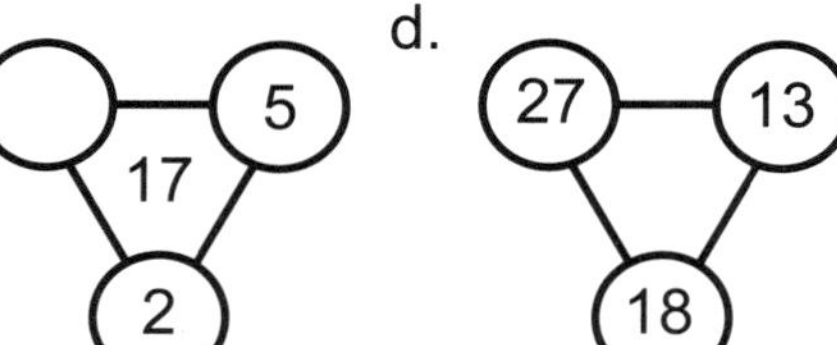

e.

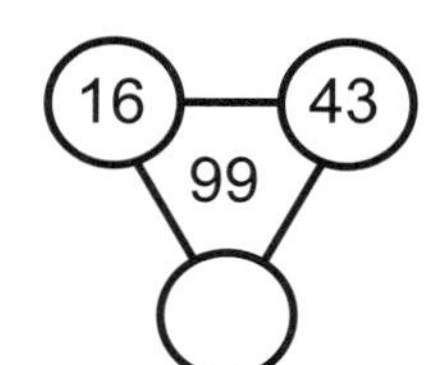

2. Examples:

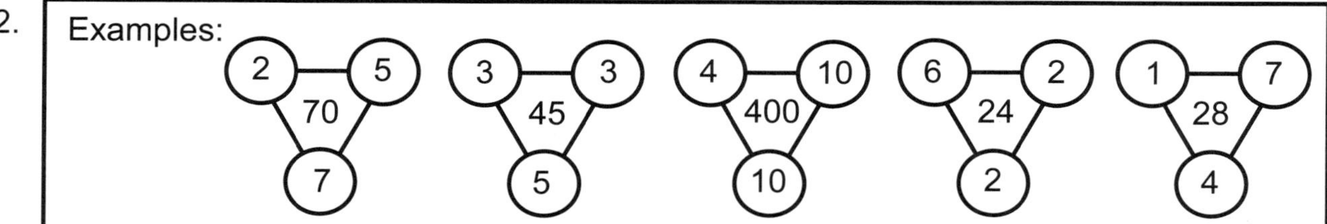

a. b.

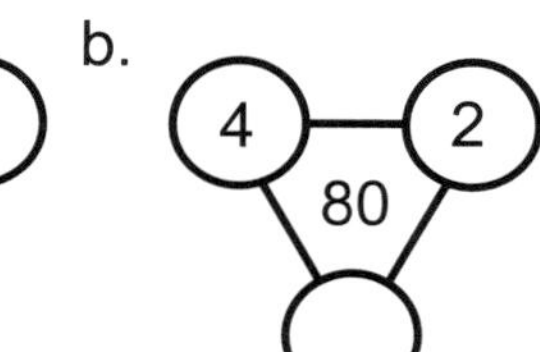

c. d.

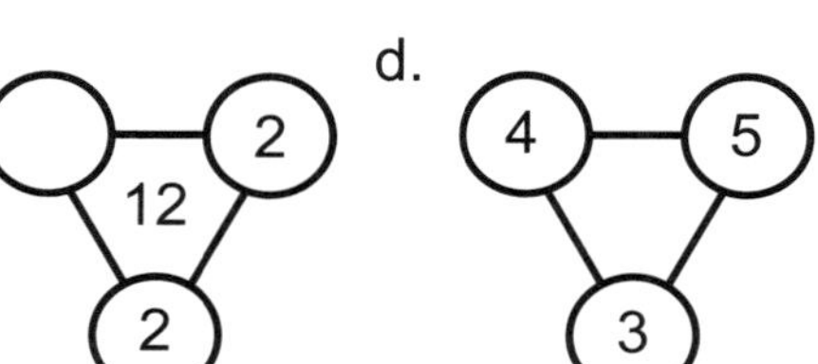

e.

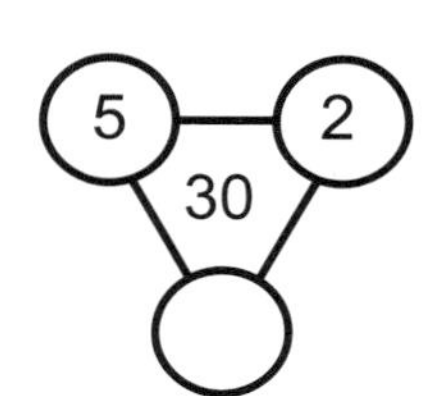

3. Examples:

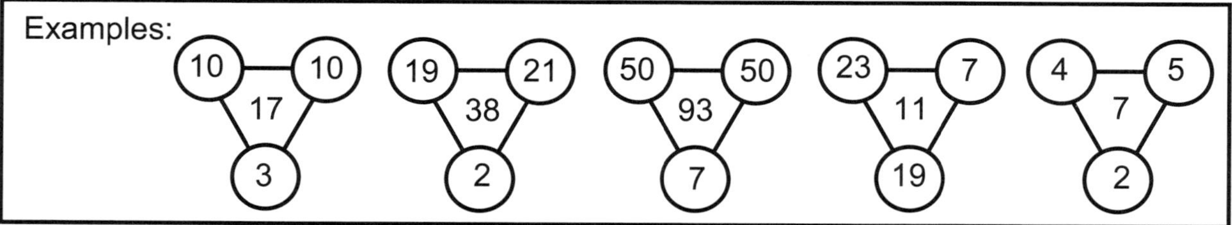

a.

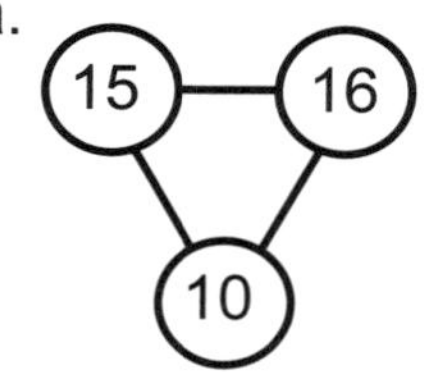

b. c.

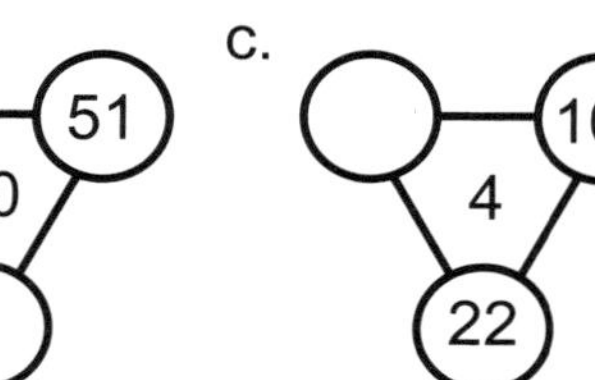

d.

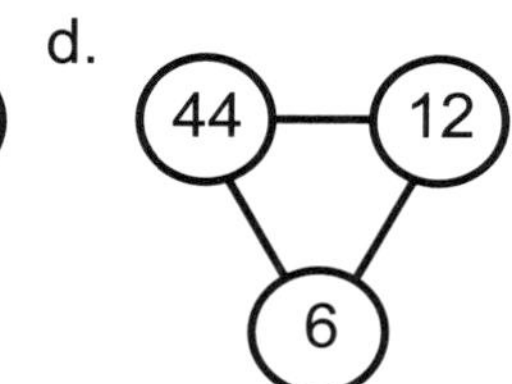

e.

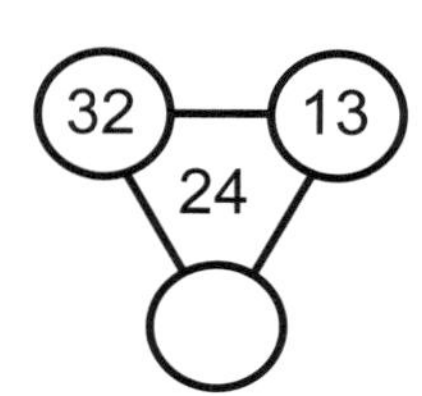

11. Pattern Predictor 3

1. Look at the pattern and then draw stage 4. For later stages, make a drawing if it helps you answer the questions.

stage 4

2. How many triangles are there at stage 4?

3. How many triangles are there at stage 5?

4. How many triangles are there at stage 6?

5. How many triangles are there at stage 7?

6. How many triangles are there at <u>stage 10</u>?

11. Pattern Predictor 3 (continued)

7. Look at the pattern and then draw stage 4. For later stages, make a drawing if it helps you answer the questions.

stage 1 stage 2 stage 3 stage 4

8. How many circles are there at stage 4?

9. How many circles are there at stage 5?

10. How many circles are there at stage 6? Complete the table to show the number of circles for stages 1 through 6.

stage	1	2	3	4	5	6
number of circles	5					

11. How many circles are there at stage 7?

12. How many circles are there at <u>stage 10</u>?

13. At what stage will there be 40 circles?

14. At what stage will there be 75 circles?

12. Equality Explorer 3

Use the numbers on the right to fill in the boxes to make the equation true. Use each number only once.

1. ☐ + ☐ = 16 + ☐ 7, 10, 13

2. ☐ + ☐ = 9 × ☐ 4, 6, 30

3. ☐ + ☐ = 20 ÷ ☐ 2, 4, 6

4. ☐ × ☐ = ☐ − ☐ 3, 7, 9, 30

5. ☐ − ☐ = ☐ ÷ ☐ 2, 3, 6, 12

6. ☐ + ☐ + 5 = ☐ + ☐ 6, 12, 13, 14

7. ☐ ÷ ☐ = ☐ + ☐ 2, 4, 6, 36

8. ☐ + ☐ + ☐ = 2 × ☐ 6, 8, 10, 12

9. ☐ + ☐ + ☐ = ☐ + ☐ 3, 5, 6, 8, 10

10. ☐ + ☐ + ☐ = ☐ × ☐ 4, 6, 7, 8, 9

13. Sequence Sleuth 3

Fill in the missing times to complete the sequence. Make sure to draw the clock hands.

1.

7:30 am	7:55 am	8:20 am		9:10 am	

2.

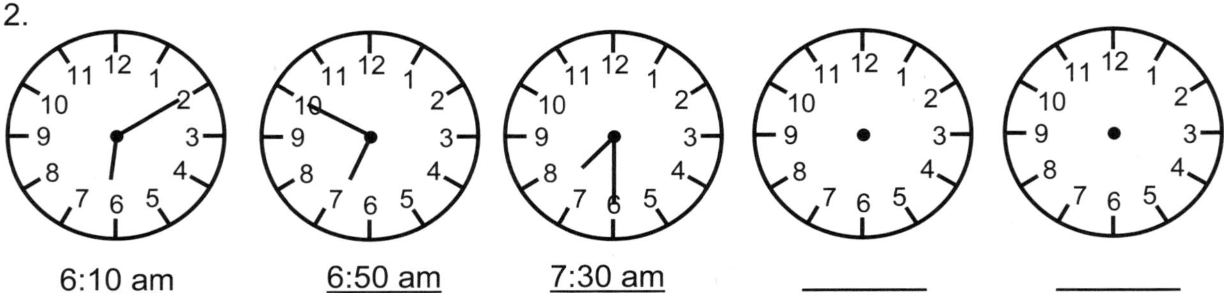

6:10 am   6:50 am   7:30 am   ______   ______

3.

11:00 am	12:15 pm	1:30 pm		4:00 pm	

4.

1:30 pm   3:00 pm   4:30 pm   ______   ______

5.

6:22 pm	6:40 pm	6:58 pm		7:34 pm	

6.

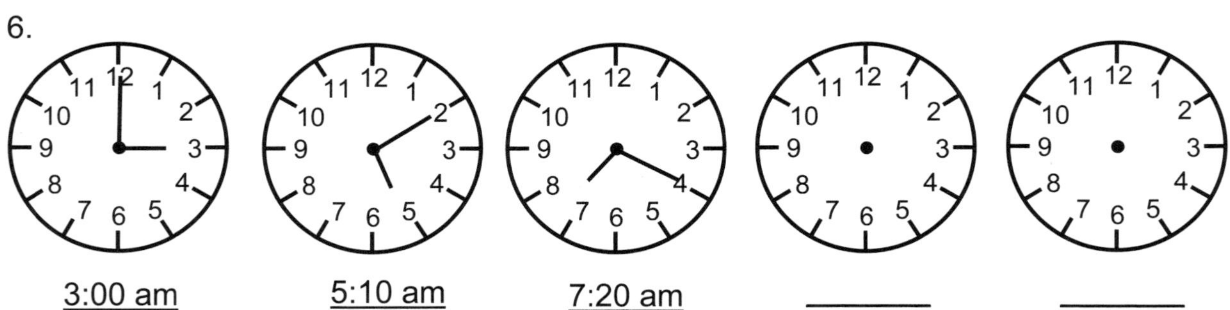

3:00 am   5:10 am   7:20 am   ______   ______

14. Number Ninja 3

The top circle's number equals the product of the numbers in the squares: 28 = 4 x 7. The bottom circle's number equals the sum of the numbers in the squares: 11 = 4 + 7.

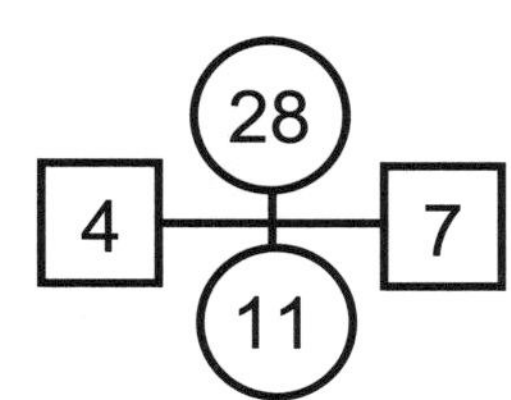

Fill in all missing numbers. When both squares are empty, put the larger of the two missing numbers in the right square.

1. 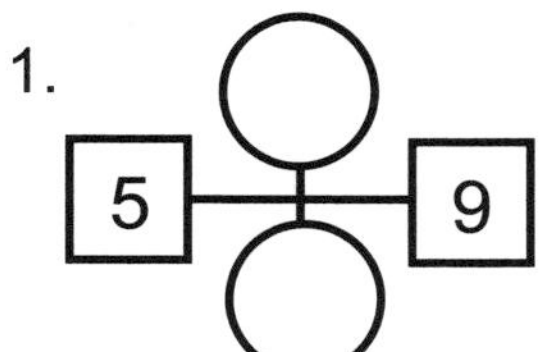

2. 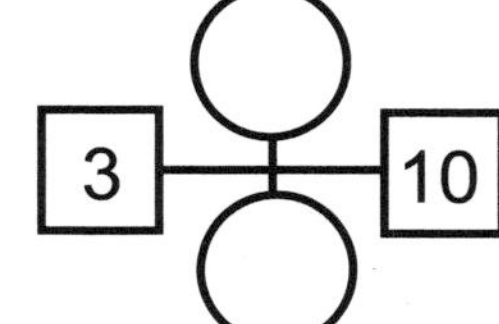

3. 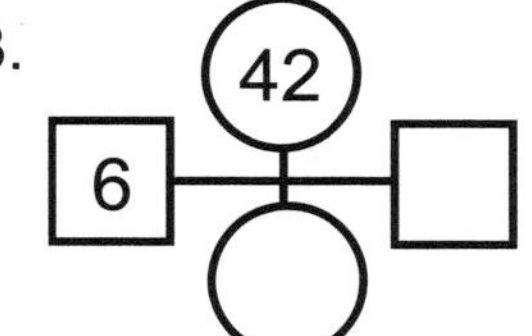

4. 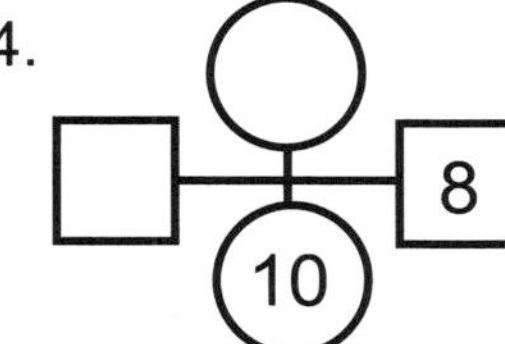

5. 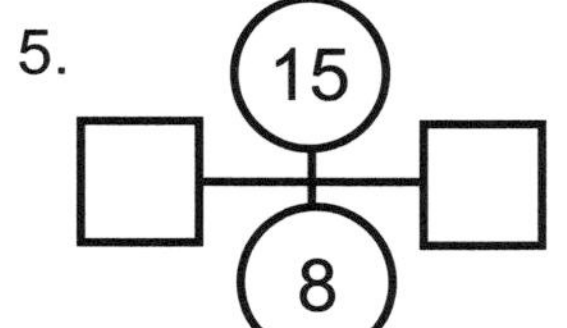

6. 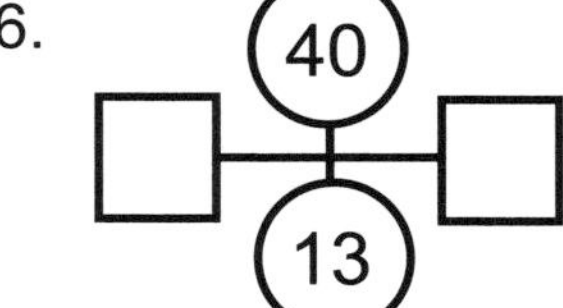

7. 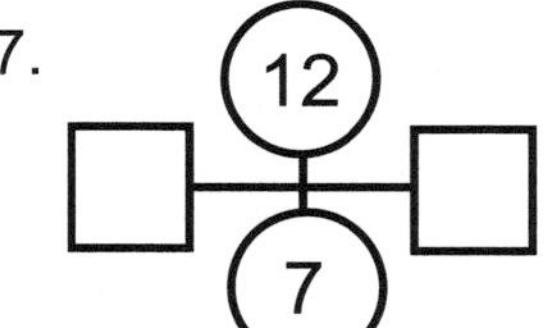

8. 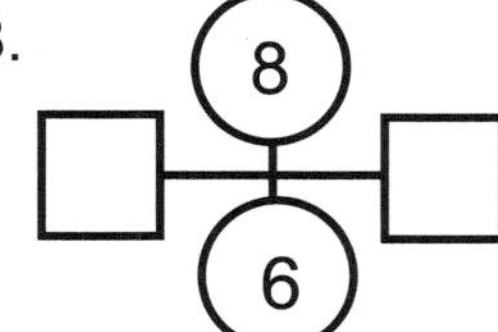

9. 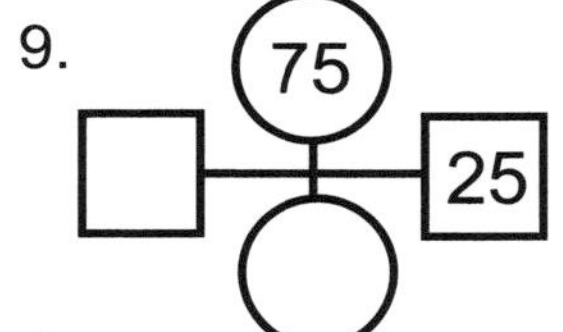

10. 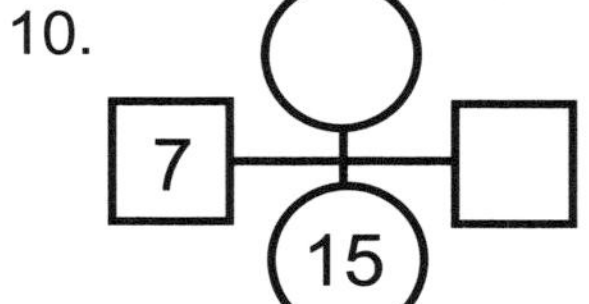

11. 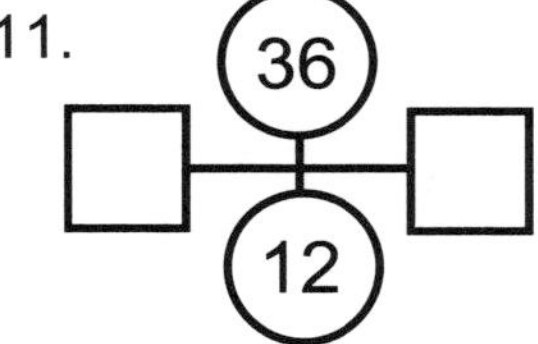

12. 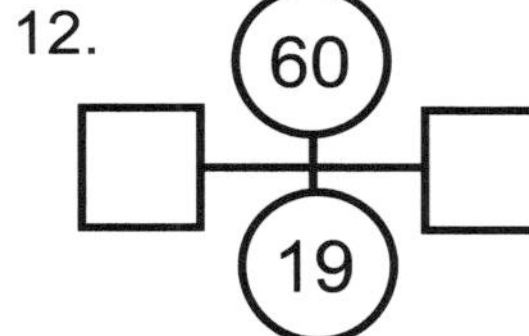

13. 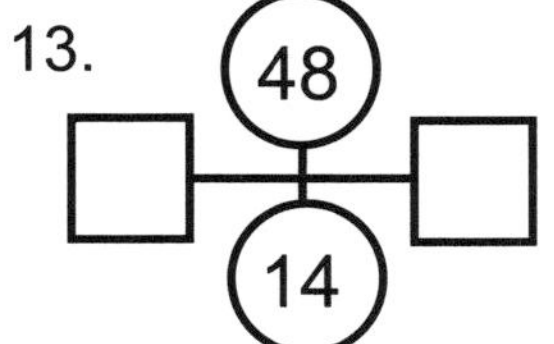

14. 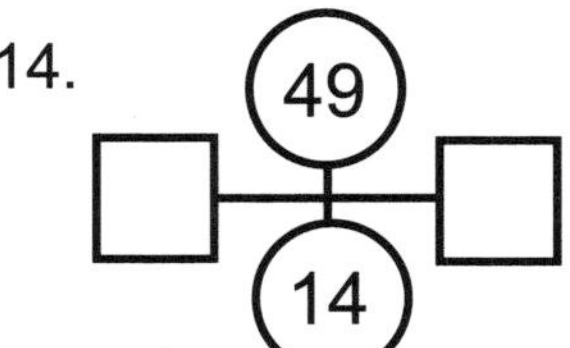

15. 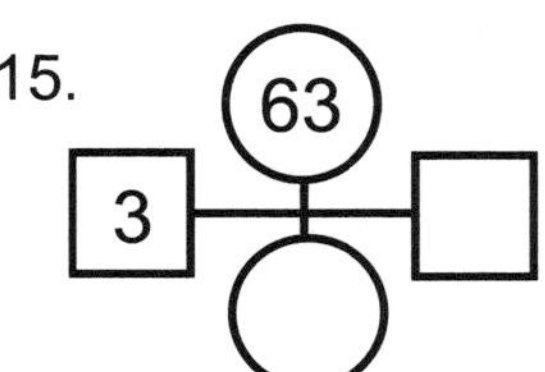

16. 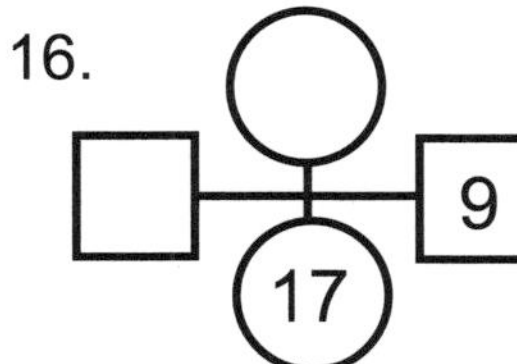

17. 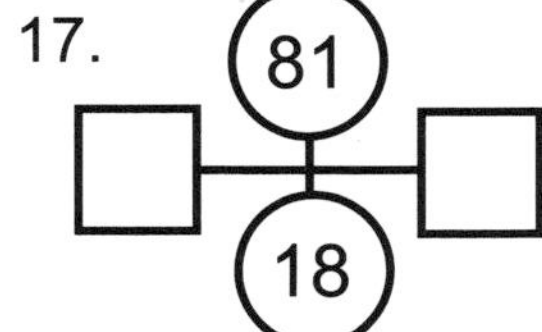

18. 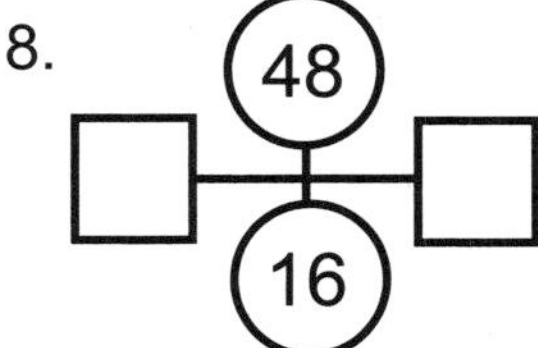

19. 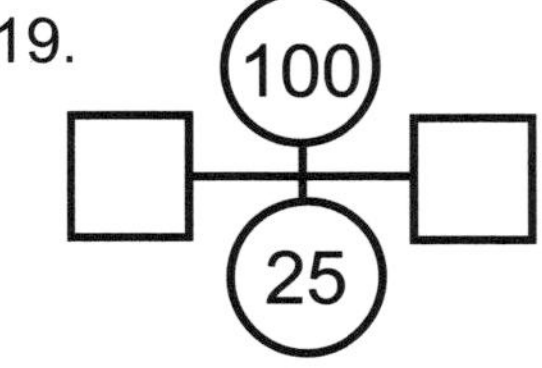

20. 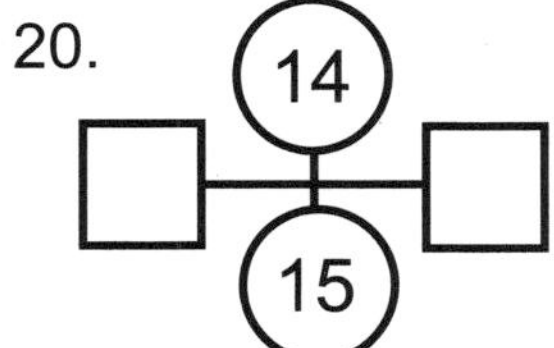

15. Function Finder 3

The function machine adds 6. So when you input 11, the output is 17.

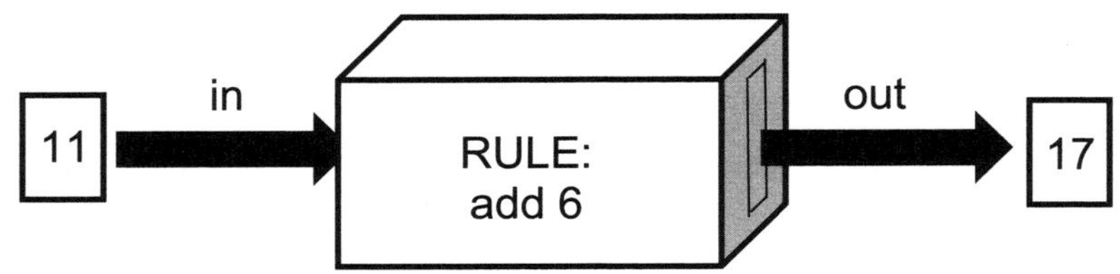

1. If you input 47, what is the output?

2. If the output is 80, what is the input?

3. Use the function machine rule to complete the table.

a. RULE: add 12

in	out
3	15
9	
18	30
	44
37	
	100

b. RULE: multiply by 3

in	out
4	12
7	
11	33
	45
20	
	90

c. RULE: subtract 9

in	out
14	5
22	
34	25
	41
67	
	84

d. RULE: divide by 4

in	out
12	3
20	
28	7
	12
60	
	22

e. RULE: add 17

in	out
5	22
13	
19	36
	48
46	
	93

f. RULE: multiply by 6

in	out
2	12
5	
8	48
	60
12	
	96

16. Pattern Predictor 4

The shapes below are made with toothpicks and gumdrops. For example, stage 2 has 5 toothpicks and 4 gumdrops.

1. Look at the pattern and then draw stage 5. For later stages, make a drawing if it helps you answer the questions.

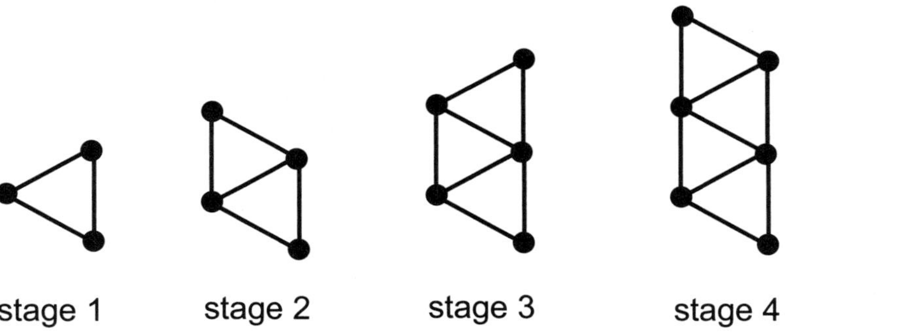

2. How many toothpicks are there at stage 5?

3. How many gumdrops are there at stage 5?

4. How many toothpicks and gumdrops are there at stage 6?

    • toothpicks: _____

    • gumdrops: _____

5. Complete the table to show the number of toothpicks and gumdrops for stages 1 through 8.

stage	1	2	3	4	5	6	7	8
number of toothpicks		5						
number of gumdrops		4						

6. How many toothpicks and gumdrops are there at stage 12?

    • toothpicks: _____

    • gumdrops: _____

16. Pattern Predictor 4 (continued)

7. Look at the pattern and then draw stage 4. For later stages, make a drawing if it helps you answer the questions.

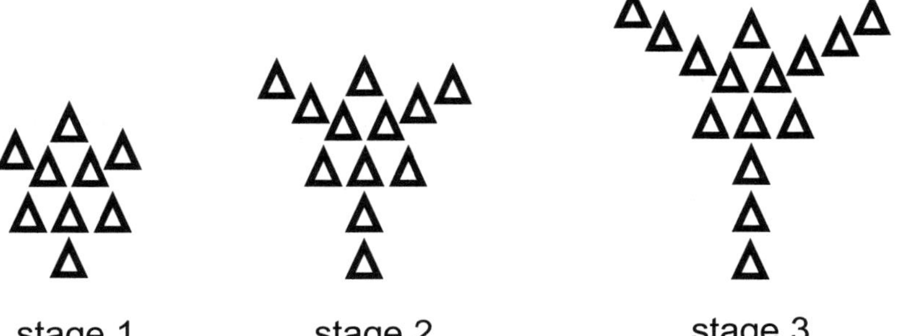

stage 1 stage 2 stage 3 stage 4

8. How many triangles are there at stage 4?

9. How many triangles are there at stage 5?

10. How many triangles are there at stage 6 and stage 7? Complete the table to show the number of triangles for stages 1 through 7.

stage	1	2	3	4	5	6	7
number of triangles	9						

11. How many triangles are there at stage 8?

12. How many triangles are there at stage 12?

17. Equality Explorer 4

Each 2D shape represents a different whole number. The sum of the numbers is written for each row (on the right) and each column (on the bottom). Find the value of each shape.

1.

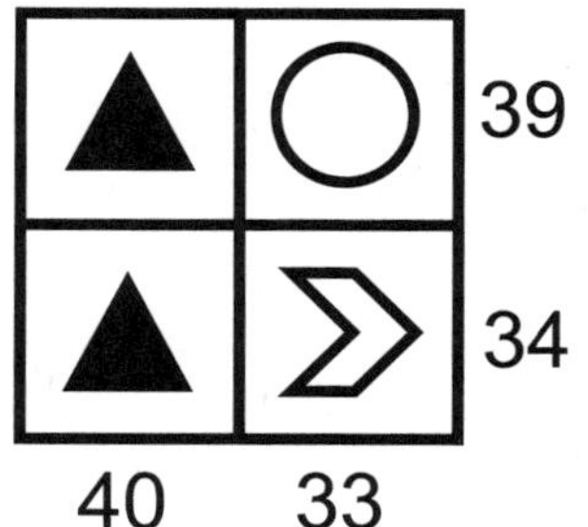

2.

3.

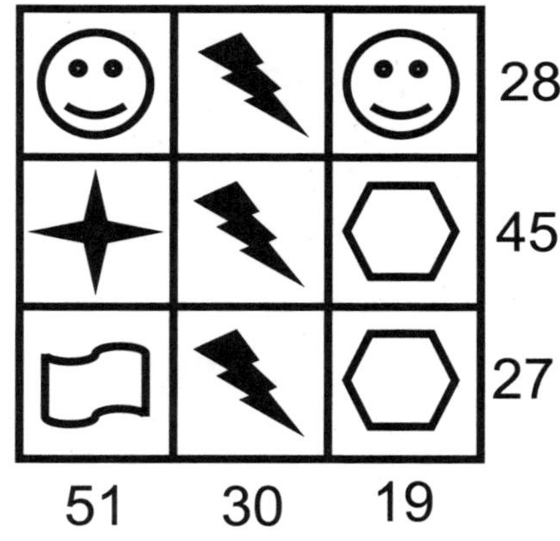

4.

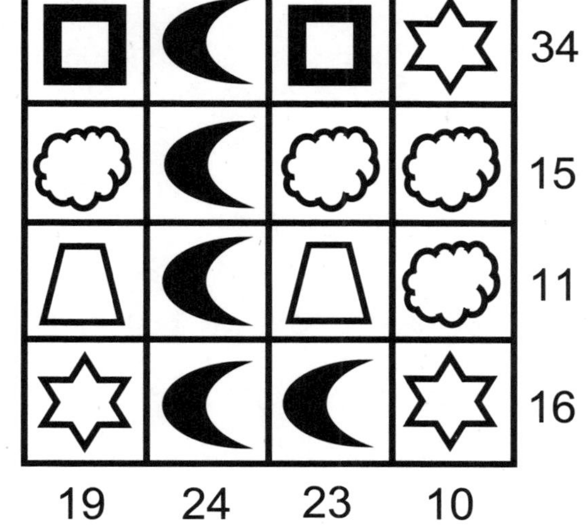

18. Sequence Sleuth 4

Create the sequence from the starting number and rule. The first one is done as an example.

1. starting number: 3	rule: multiply by 2	3, 6, 12, 24, 48
2. starting number: 10	rule: add 25	____, ____, ____, ____, ____
3. starting number: 80	rule: divide by 2	____, ____, ____, ____, ____
4. starting number: 99	rule: subtract 7	____, ____, ____, ____, ____
5. starting number: 1	rule: multiply by 3	____, ____, ____, ____, ____
6. starting number: 32	rule: add 8	____, ____, ____, ____, ____

State the starting number and rule for the sequence. The first one is done as an example.

7. 115, 105, 95, 85, 75, 65	starting number: 115	rule: subtract 10
8. 25, 37, 49, 61, 73, 85	starting number: ____	rule: ____________
9. 15, 30, 60, 120, 240, 480	starting number: ____	rule: ____________
10. 50, 46, 42, 38, 34, 30	starting number: ____	rule: ____________
11. 64, 32, 16, 8, 4, 2	starting number: ____	rule: ____________
12. 19, 27, 35, 43, 51, 59	starting number: ____	rule: ____________

19. Number Ninja 4

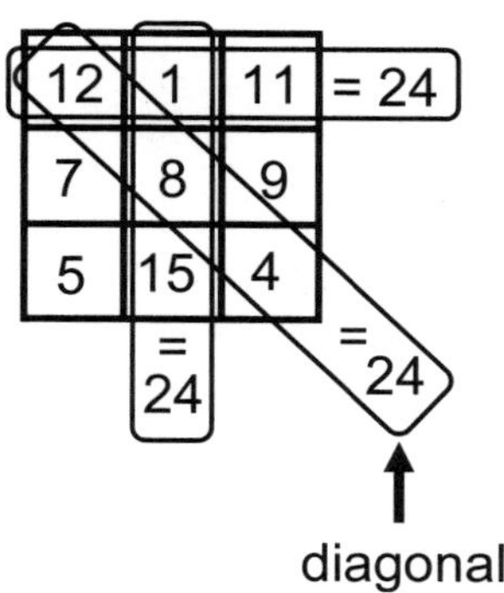

In a Magic Square the numbers in each row, column, and diagonal add up to the same number. For the example shown, the sum for each row, column, and diagonal is 24.

Fill in all empty squares to create magic squares with the indicated sums. Remember to check the sum for each of the square's two diagonals.

1.

sum = 18

9		7
		3

2.

sum = 30

	10	
9		13

3.

sum = 21

8		
	7	11

4.

sum = 40

19			3
	12		13
6		1	
10	7		

5.

sum = 24

	7	9	5
	6	2	
3	7		5

6.

sum = 70

30		14	
	16		
	23		21
9		25	19

20. Function Finder 4

Each question gives 5 examples of 4 numbers in a square related by a secret pattern. Discover the pattern and then fill in the missing numbers.

1. Examples:

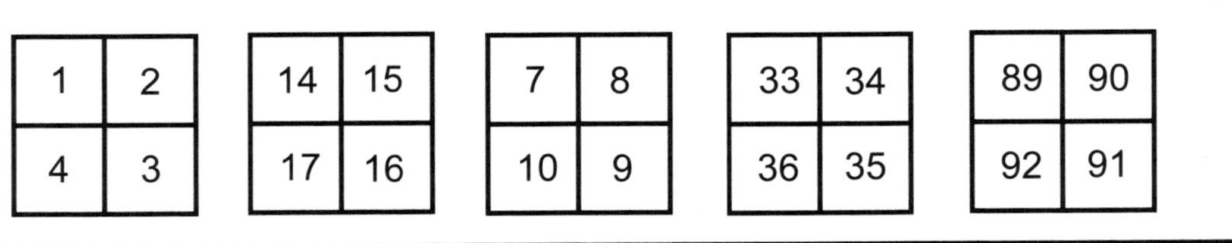

1	2
4	3

14	15
17	16

7	8
10	9

33	34
36	35

89	90
92	91

a.

60	61
	62

b.

25	
28	27

c.

73	
	75

d.

	49
51	

e.

67	
70	

2. Examples:

13	16
22	19

75	78
84	81

51	54
60	57

29	32
38	35

4	7
13	10

a.

22	
31	28

b.

47	50
56	

c.

38	
	44

d.

80	
89	

e.

	9
15	

3. Examples:

18	25
39	32

52	59
73	66

3	10
24	17

34	41
55	48

80	87
101	94

a.

12	19
	26

b.

44	51
65	

c.

36	
	50

d.

	78
	85

e.

65	
86	

21. Pattern Predictor 5

The shapes below are made with toothpicks and gumdrops. For example, stage 2 has 7 toothpicks and 6 gumdrops.

1. Look at the pattern and then draw stage 4. For later stages, make a drawing if it helps you answer the questions.

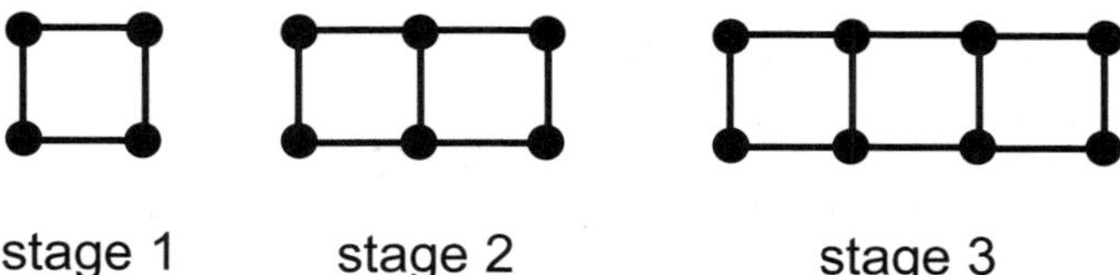

stage 1 stage 2 stage 3 stage 4

2. How many toothpicks are there at stage 4?

3. How many gumdrops are there at stage 4?

4. How many toothpicks and gumdrops are there at stage 5?

   - toothpicks: _____
   - gumdrops: _____

5. Complete the table to show the number of toothpicks and gumdrops for stages 1 through 7.

stage	1	2	3	4	5	6	7
number of toothpicks		7					
number of gumdrops		6					

6. What is the number of toothpicks and gumdrops at stage 9?

   - toothpicks: _____
   - gumdrops: _____

21. Pattern Predictor 5 (continued)

7. Look at the pattern and then draw stage 4. For later stages, make a drawing if it helps you answer the questions.

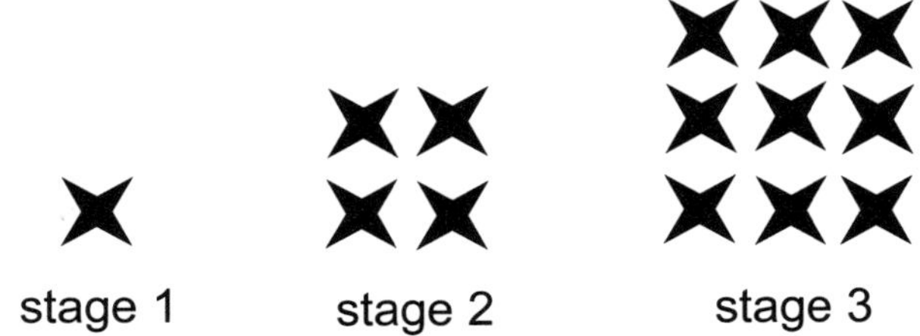

stage 4

8. How many stars are there at stage 4?

9. How many stars are there at stage 5?

10. How many stars are there at stage 6?

11. How many stars are there at stage 7?

12. How many stars are there at <u>stage 10</u>?

22. Equality Explorer 5

Each 2D shape represents a different whole number. Use the equations to find their value.

1. ⬠ × ♥ = 36
   ⬠ + ⬠ = 8

   ⬠ = ___ ♥ = ___

2. ☁ − ⏢ = 1
   ☁ × ⏢ = 30

   ☁ = ___ ⏢ = ___

3. ★ + ☾ + ☾ = 17
   ★ × ☾ = 21

   ★ = ___ ☾ = ___

4. ✡ ÷ ☺ = 4
   ✡ + ☺ = 10

   ✡ = ___ ☺ = ___

5. △ + △ + 6 = 30
   ⚡ + ⚡ − △ = 8
   ▱ × ⚡ = 130

   △ = ___ ⚡ = ___ ▱ = ___

6. 30 ÷ ◆ = 2
   4 + □ = ◆
   ✦ + □ + ◆ = 40

   ✦ = ___ □ = ___ ◆ = ___

23. Sequence Sleuth 5

Circle all remaining numbers that belong in the sequence.

1.

1	2	**3**	4	5
6	7	8	**9**	10
11	**12**	13	14	15
16	17	18	19	20
21	22	23	24	25
26	27	28	29	30
31	32	33	34	35
36	37	38	39	40
41	42	43	44	45
46	47	48	49	50

2.

1	2	3	**4**	5	6
7	**8**	9	10	11	**12**
13	14	15	**16**	17	18
19	20	21	22	23	24
25	26	27	28	29	30
31	32	33	34	35	36
37	38	39	40	41	42
43	44	45	46	47	48
49	50	51	52	53	54
55	56	57	58	59	60

3.

1	2	3	4	5	**6**
7	8	9	10	**11**	12
13	14	15	**16**	17	18
19	20	21	22	23	24
25	26	27	28	29	30
31	32	33	34	35	36
37	38	39	40	41	42
43	44	45	46	47	48
49	50	51	52	53	54
55	56	57	58	59	60

4.

1	2	**3**	4	**5**
6	**7**	8	9	10
11	12	13	14	15
16	17	18	19	20
21	22	23	24	25
26	27	28	29	30
31	32	33	34	35
36	37	38	39	40
41	42	43	44	45
46	47	48	49	50

5.

1	2	**3**	4	5	6
7	8	9	**10**	11	12
13	14	15	16	**17**	18
19	20	21	22	23	**24**
25	26	27	28	29	30
31	32	33	34	35	36
37	38	39	40	41	42
43	44	45	46	47	48
49	50	51	52	53	54
55	56	57	58	59	60

6.

1	**2**	3	4	5
6	7	8	9	**10**
11	12	13	**14**	15
16	17	18	19	20
21	22	23	24	25
26	27	28	29	30
31	32	33	34	35
36	37	38	39	40
41	42	43	44	45
46	47	48	49	50

7.

1	2	**3**	4	5	6	7	8
9	10	11	12	13	14	**15**	16
17	18	19	20	**21**	22	23	24
25	26	27	28	29	30	31	32
33	34	35	36	37	38	39	40
41	42	43	44	45	46	47	48
49	50	51	52	53	54	55	56
57	58	59	60	61	62	63	64
65	66	67	68	69	70	71	72
73	74	75	76	77	78	79	80

8.

1	2	**3**	4	5	**6**	7	8	**9**	10
11	**12**	13	14	15	16	17	18	19	20
21	22	23	24	25	26	27	28	29	30
31	32	33	34	35	36	37	38	39	40
41	42	43	44	45	46	47	48	49	50
51	52	53	54	55	56	57	58	59	60
61	62	63	64	65	66	67	68	69	70
71	72	73	74	75	76	77	78	79	80
81	82	83	84	85	86	87	88	89	90
91	92	93	94	95	96	97	98	99	100

24. Number Ninja 5

Each number is the sum of the 2 numbers directly below it. Use this rule to fill in all the empty spaces.

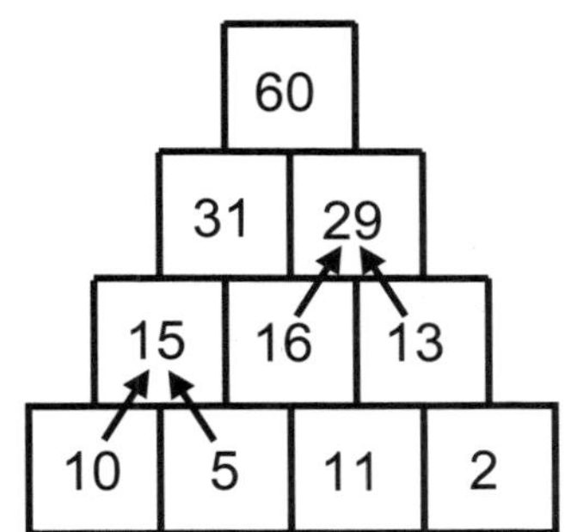

1.

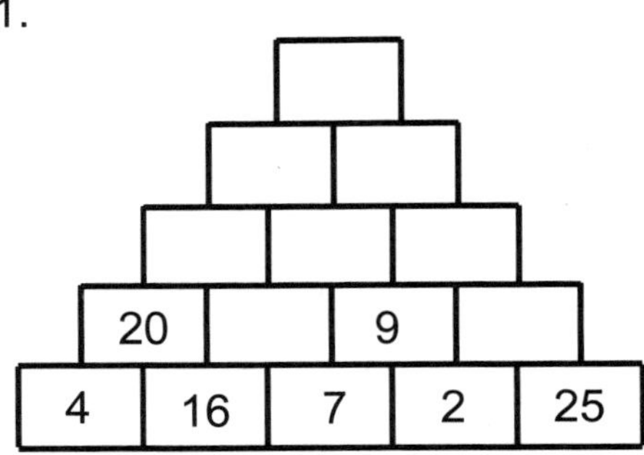

2.

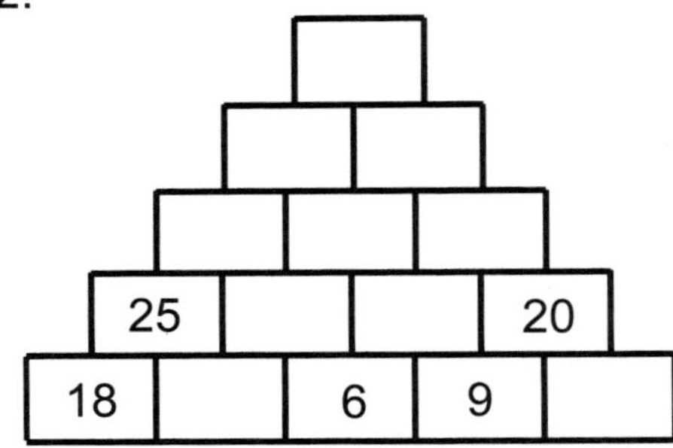

3.

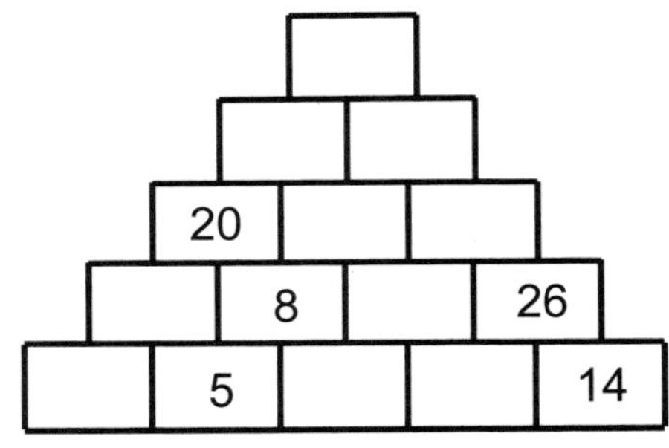

4.

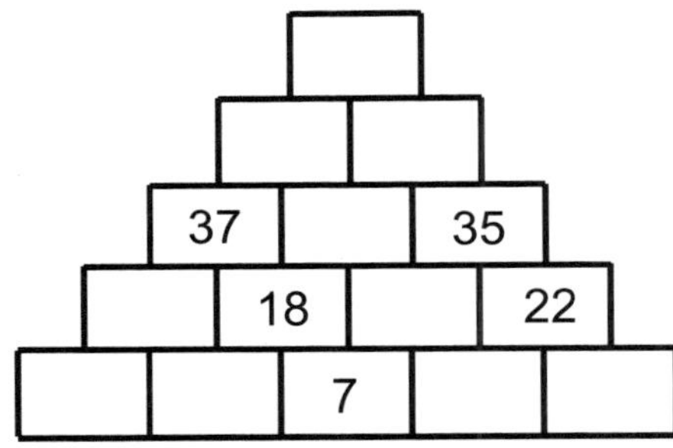

5.

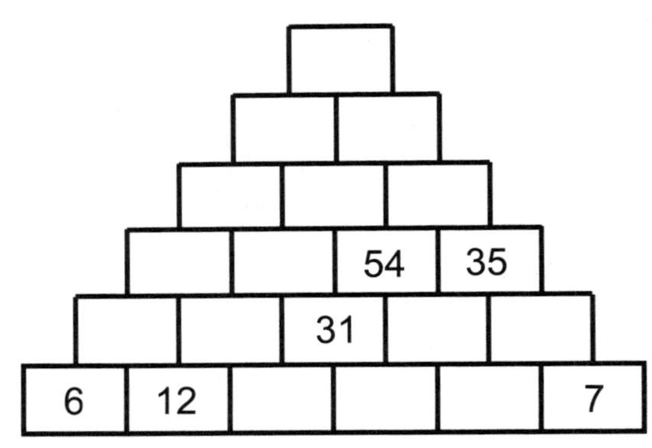

6.

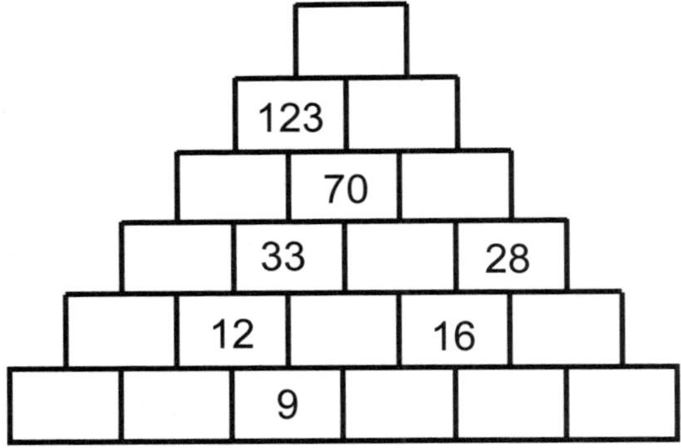

25. Function Finder 5

1. The function machine multiplies by 7. So when you input 5, the output is 35. Use the rule to complete the table.

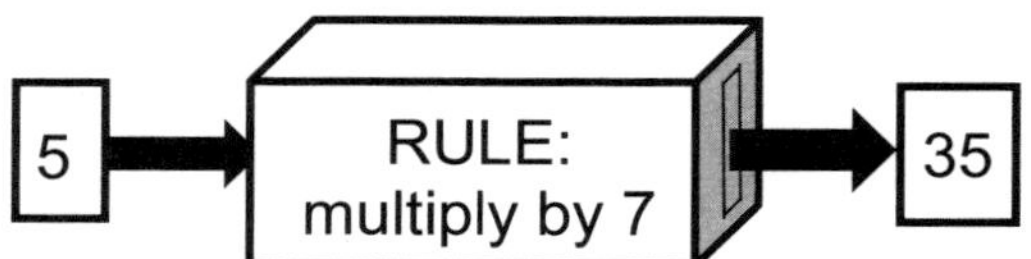

in	2	5	7	11		30
out	14	35	49		140	

2. Complete the table and state the function machine rule.

a. RULE: ______________________

in	2	6	9	13		32
out	10	30	45		100	

b. RULE: ______________________

in	2	5	8	12		22
out	6	15	24		48	

3a. Complete the table.

gallons	3	5	9	12		25
quarts	12	20	36		80	

b. A car holds 15 gallons of gasoline. How many quarts is this?

c. A water tank holds 40 quarts of water. How many gallons is this?

4a. Complete the table.

feet	2	3	5	7		15
inches	24	36	60		120	

b. Stephanie is 4 feet tall. How many inches is this?

c. Brett is 72 inches tall. How many feet is this?

5a. Complete the table.

tickets	1	2	5	8	11		18
cost (dollars)	6	12	30	48		90	

b. Lenny buys 9 tickets. How many dollars does this cost?

c. Mabel spends $42 on tickets. How many tickets does she buy?

26. Pattern Predictor 6

The shapes below are made with toothpicks and gumdrops. For example, stage 2 has 9 toothpicks and 8 gumdrops.

1. Look at the pattern and then draw stage 4. For later stages, make a drawing if it helps you answer the questions.

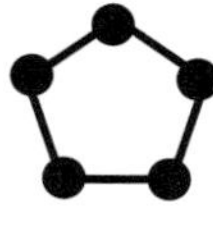

stage 1

stage 2

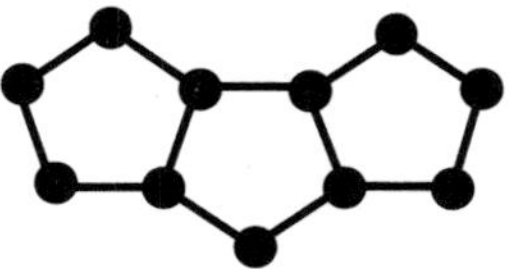

stage 3

stage 4

2. How many toothpicks ╲ are there at stage 4?

3. How many gumdrops ● are there at stage 4?

4. How many toothpicks and gumdrops are there at stage 5?

- toothpicks: _____
- gumdrops: _____

5. Complete the table to show the number of toothpicks and gumdrops for stages 1 through 7.

stage	1	2	3	4	5	6	7
number of toothpicks		9					
number of gumdrops		8					

6. What is the number of toothpicks and gumdrops at stage 10?

- toothpicks: _____
- gumdrops: _____

26. Pattern Predictor 6 (continued)

7. Look at the pattern and then draw stage 5. For later stages, make a drawing if it helps you answer the questions.

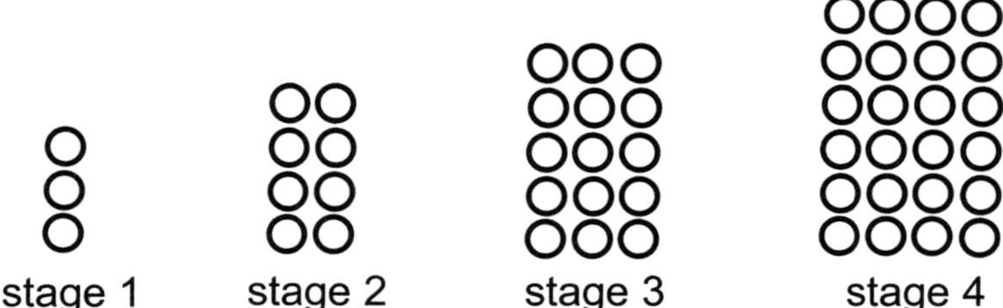

stage 5

8. How many circles are there at stage 5?

9. How many circles are there at stage 6?

10. How many circles are there at stage 7?

11. How many circles are there at stage 8?

12. How many circles are there at <u>stage 11</u>?

27. Equality Explorer 6

Write whole numbers in the empty boxes to make the numbers add up to the sum for each row (written on the right) and each column (written on the bottom).

1.

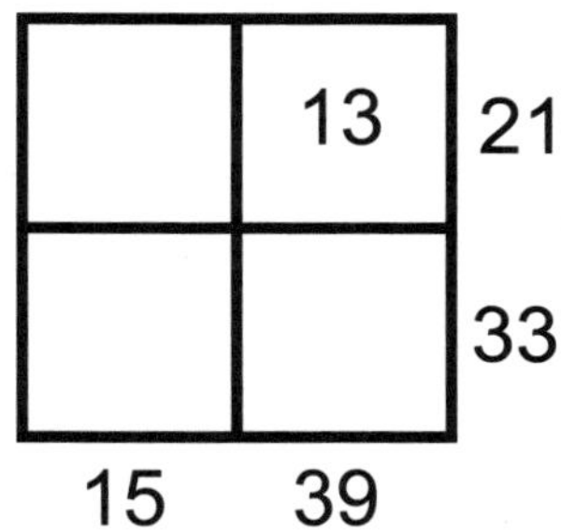

	13	21
		33
15	39	

2.

		5	29
9			31
21	17		44
33	48	23	

3.

	7	19	11	47
13			4	35
		18	25	56
6	9			33
37	37	42	55	

4.

13		16	6	55
		15		38
	2	9	4	29
7			10	45
37	39	63	28	

28. Sequence Sleuth 6

1. a. Find the pattern and draw shape 9.

b. Draw shape 11. c. Draw shape 15. d. Draw shape 18.

2. a. Find the pattern and draw shape 11.

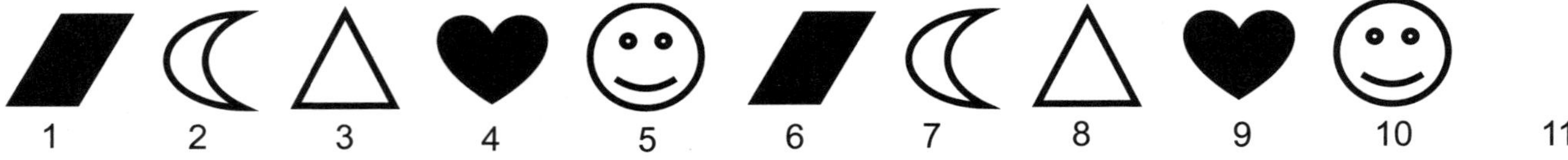

b. Draw shape 12. c. Draw shape 16. d. Draw shape 20.

3. a. Find the pattern and draw shape 9.

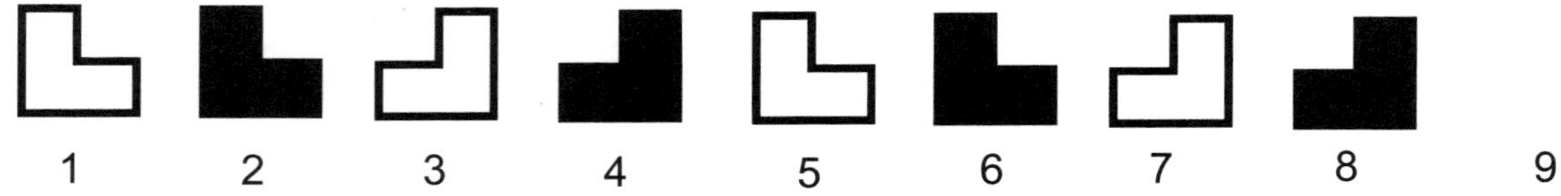

b . Draw shape 12. c. Draw shape 16. d. Draw shape 21.

4. a. Find the pattern and then write letters 12 through 16.

A	B	B	C	C	C	D	D	D	D	E					
1	2	3	4	5	6	7	8	9	10	11	12	13	14	15	16

b. Write letter 23. c. Write letter 31.

29. Number Ninja 6

Put the numbers 1, 2, 3, 4, 5, 6 into the circles so that each side of the triangle adds up to the indicated sum. Use each number only once. For each triangle, one or more numbers have already been placed in the circles.

1. sum = 9

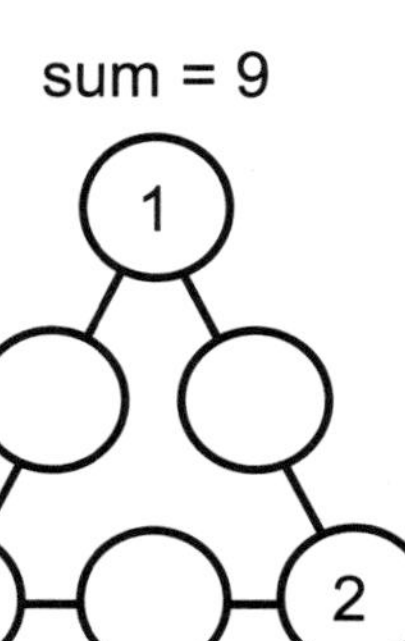

2. sum = 10

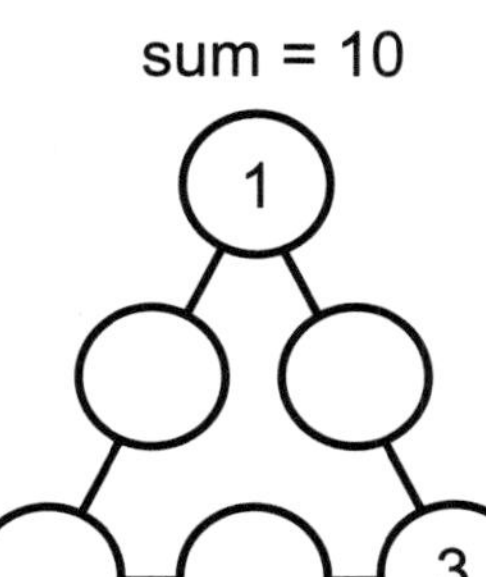

3. sum = 11

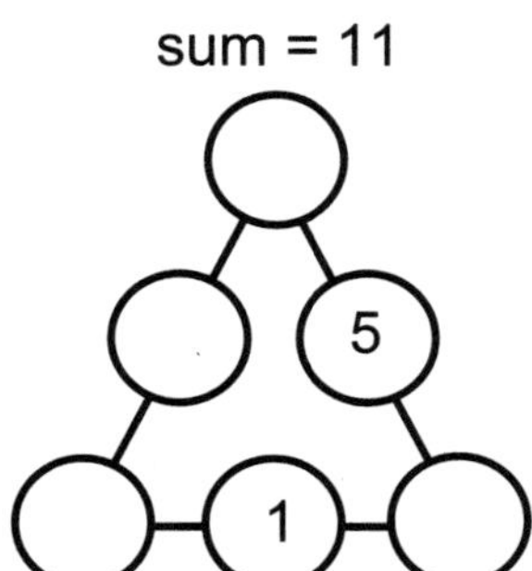

4. sum = 12

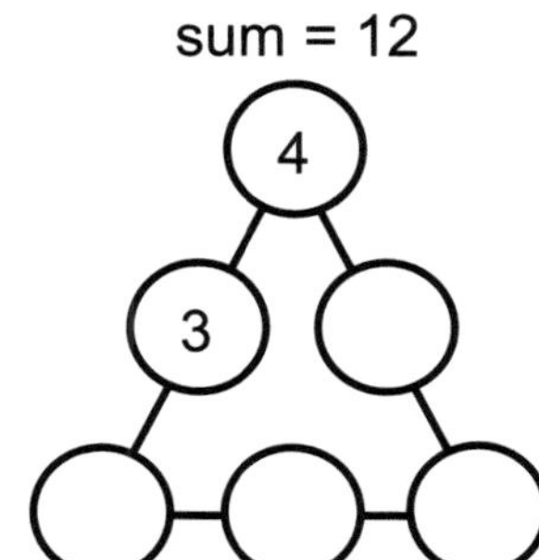

Put the numbers 1, 2, 3, 4, 5, 6, 7, 8, 9 into the circles so that each side of the triangle adds up to the indicated sum. Use each number only once. For each triangle, one or more numbers have already been placed in the circles.

5. sum = 17

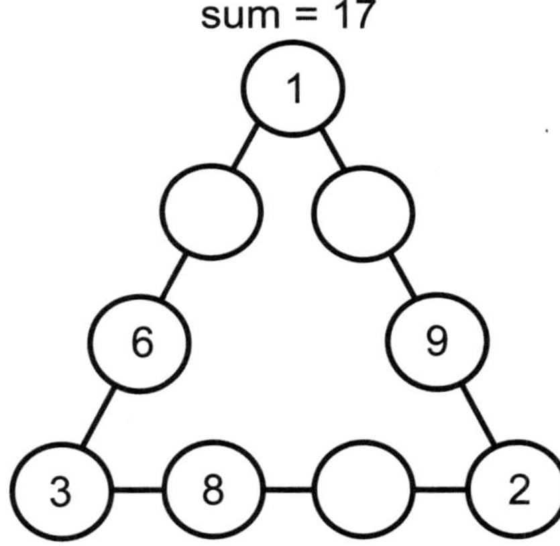

6. sum = 19

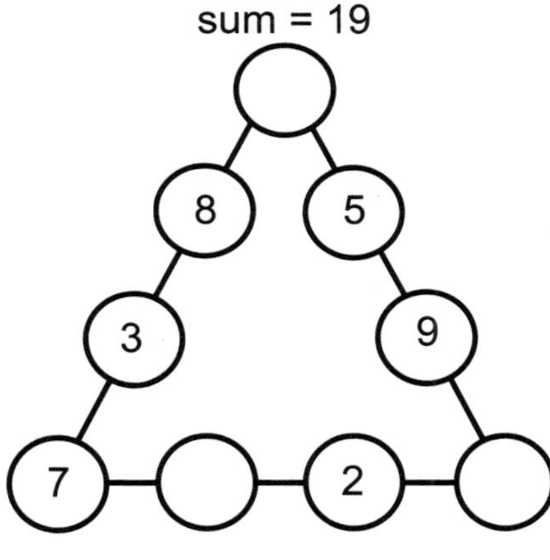

7. sum = 23

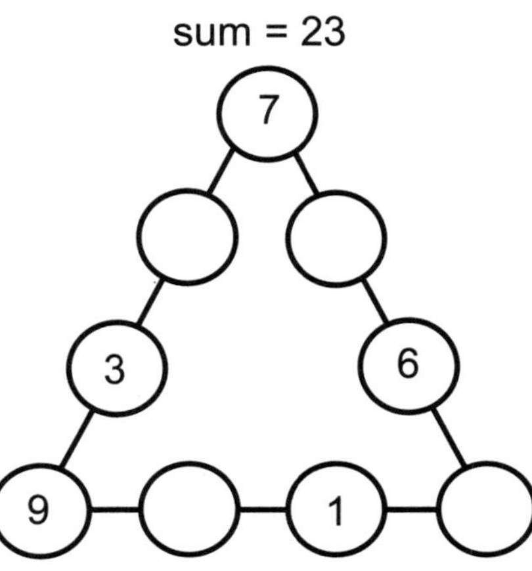

8. sum = 21

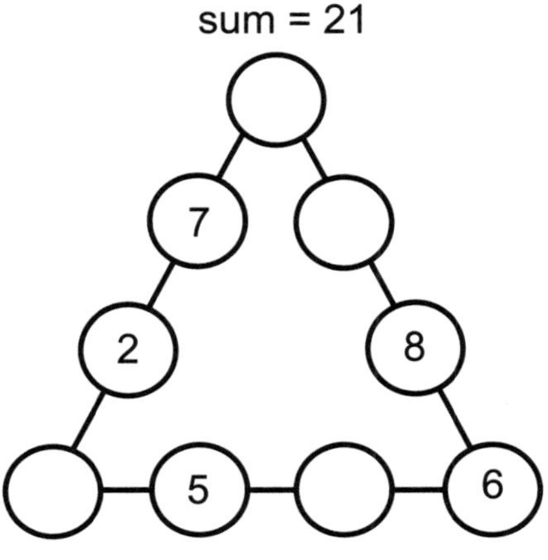

30. Function Finder 6

1. The function machine adds 13. So when you input 9, the output is 22. Use the rule to complete the table.

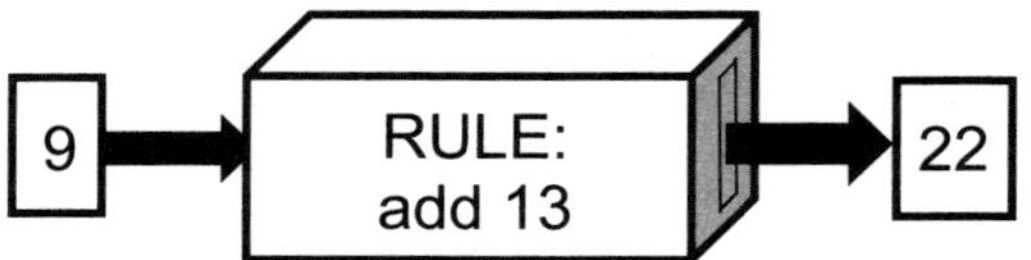

in	4	9	16	21		54
out	17	22	29		45	

2. Complete the table and state the function machine rule.

a. RULE: ______________________

in	14	21	29	36		74
out	24	31	39		52	

b. RULE: ______________________

in	6	13	18	25		57
out	28	35	40		64	

3a. Complete the table.

Spencer's age	5	11	23	35		66
Amanda's age	13	19	31		52	

b. Spencer is 16. How old is Amanda?

c. Amanda is 47. How old is Spencer?

4a. Complete the table.

cost to make cake ($)	6	9	15	22	28	
selling price of cake ($)	11	14	20	27		41

b. It costs $25 to make the cake.
What is the selling price of the cake?

c. The selling price of the cake is $17.
How much does it cost to make the cake?

5a. Complete the table.

Sammy's situps	20	32	45	57	70	
Sammy's pushups	5	17	30	42		88

b. Sammy does 27 situps. How many pushups does he do?

c. Sammy does 50 pushups.
How many situps does he do?

31. Pattern Predictor 7

1. Look at the pattern and then draw stage 4. For later stages, make a drawing if it helps you answer the questions.

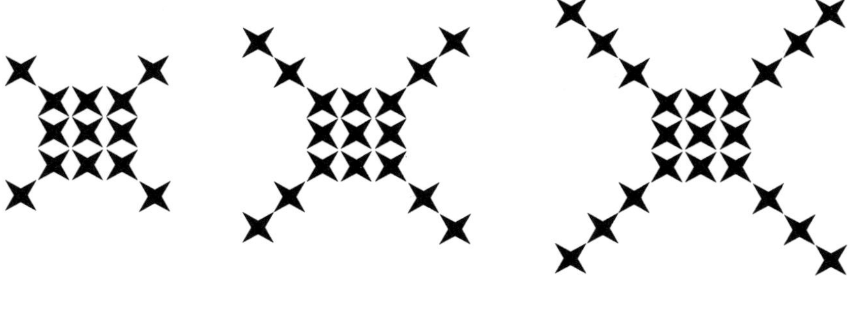

stage 1 stage 2 stage 3 stage 4

2. How many stars are there at stage 4?

3. How many stars are there at stage 5?

4. How many stars are there at stage 6 and stage 7? Complete the table to show the number of stars for stages 1 through 7.

stage	1	2	3	4	5	6	7
number of stars	13						

5. How many stars are there at stage 8?

6. How many stars are there at stage 12?

31. Pattern Predictor 7 (continued)

7. Look at the pattern and then draw stage 4. For later stages, make a drawing if it helps you answer the questions.

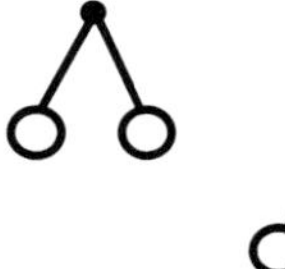

stage 1

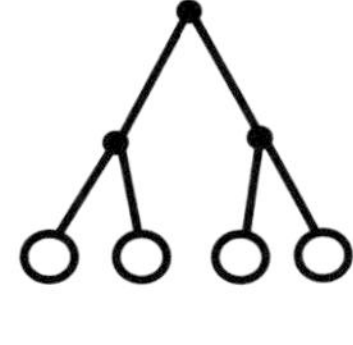

stage 2

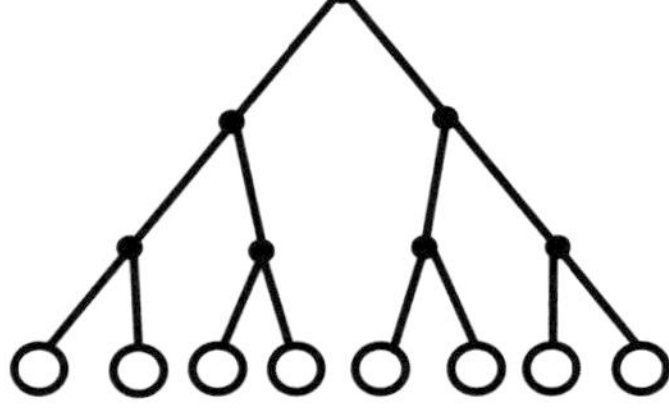

stage 3

stage 4

8. Determine how many open dots O there are at stage 4 and then complete the table summarizing your results.

stage	number of open dots
1	2
2	4
3	
4	

9. Explain in words the pattern you see in the table. Then state the number of open dots in stage 5 and stage 6.

- stage 5: _____
- stage 6: _____

10. How many open dots are there at <u>stage 8</u>?

32. Equality Explorer 7

Each 2D shape represents a different whole number. Use the equations to find their value.

1.

◇ × ◇ = 25

◇ + ◇ + ◇ = ☾ + 2

◇ = __ ☾ = __

2.

⬠ × ⬠ × ⬠ = 8

⬠ × ϟ × ϟ = 18

⬠ = __ ϟ = __

3.

☺ + ◐ = 9

♡ + ♡ + ◖ = 25

☺ = __ ♡ = __

4.

✡ + ▰ = 10

✡ − ▰ = 8

✡ = __ ▰ = __

5.

☁ × ▲ = 32

☁ ÷ ▲ = 2

▲ + □ = 16

▲ = __ ☁ = __ □ = __

6.

⏢ + ⏢ − 7 = ✦

✦ ÷ 3 = 5

3 + ✦ − ⏢ = ○

⏢ = __ ✦ = __ ○ = __

33. Sequence Sleuth 7

Study the sequence in row A to discover the rule. Then apply this rule to complete the sequences in rows B, C, and D.

1.

A: 91, 85, 79, 73, 67, 61, 55, 49

B: 59, 53, 47, __ , 35, 29, __ , 17

C: 64, 58, 52, 46, __ , __ , 28, __

D: 80, 74, __ , __ , 56, 50, __ , __

2.

A: 5, 6, 8, 11, 15, 20, 26, 33

B: 22, 23, 25, 28, 32, 37, __ , 50

C: 67, 68, 70, 73, __ , 82, __ , 95

D: 39, 40, __ , 45, __ , 54, __ , 67

3.

A: 11, 15, 16, 20, 21, 25, 26, 30

B: 18, 22, 23, 27, 28, 32, __ , 37

C: 46, 50, 51, 55, __ , 60, __ , __

D: 77, 81, __ , 86, __ , __ , 92, __

4.

A: 70, 62, 60, 52, 50, 42, 40, 32

B: 85, 77, 75, 67, __ , 57, 55, __

C: 94, 86, 84, 76, __ , __ , 64, __

D: 89, 81, 79, __ , __ , 61, __ , __

5.

A: 5, 10, 20, 40, 80, 160

B: 2, 4, 8, 16, ___ , ___

C: 3, 6, 12, ___ , 48, ___

D: 7, 14, 28, ___ ,112, ___

6.

A: 40, 32, 35, 27, 30, 22, 25, 17

B: 58, 50, 53, 45, 48, 40, __ , __

C: 94, 86, 89, 81, __ , 76, __ , __

D: 73, 65, 68, __ , __ , 55, __ , __

34. Number Ninja 7

Fill in the blanks to make the equations true.

1. 27 + ____ = 9 x 7

2. 48 – ____ = 60 ÷ 4

3. 83 – 38 = 3 x ____

4. 36 ÷ ____ = 19 – 15

5. 34 + 18 = 19 + ____ + 23

6. 21 + 17 – ____ = 48 ÷ 4

7. ____ ÷ 17 = 32 ÷ 8

8. 8 x 9 = ____ x 6

9. 60 – ____ = 11 + 13 + 15

10. 77 + ____ = 104 – 18

Select from the four available numbers 2, 4, 6, 8 and put them in the blank spaces to make the equation true. For each equation, use each selected number exactly once. The first problem is done as an example.

11. 2 x 4 + 8 = 16

12. ____ + ____ – ____ = 12

13. ____ x ____ – ____ = 30

14. ____ ÷ ____ + ____ = 4

15. ____ + ____ – ____ = 8

16. ____ x ____ + ____ = 22

17. ____ x ____ x ____ = 64

18. ____ + ____ + ____ = 14

35. Function Finder 7

1a. Complete the table.

number of cheeseburgers	3	5	8	10	14		20
total cost ($)	15	25	40	50		90	100

b. What is the total cost of 30 cheeseburgers?

c. How many cheeseburgers are bought if the total cost is $60?

2a. Complete the table.

start of class	8:00 am	9:15 am	10:20 am	1:30 pm	3:25 pm		8:05 pm
end of class	8:40 am	9:55 am	11:00 am	2:10 pm		5:20 pm	8:45 pm

b. If class starts at 11:45 am, when does it end?

c. If class ends at 3:10 pm, when does it start?

3a. Complete the table.

number of minutes walking	1	5	8	20	30		50
number of calories burned	4	20	32	80		160	200

b. 25 minutes of walking burns how many calories?

c. How many minutes of walking are needed to burn 48 calories?

4a. Complete the table.

teacher's age	28	35	42	50	57		68
number of years teaching	6	13	20	28		40	46

b. If the teacher is 45 years old, how many years has she taught?

c. If the teacher has taught for 9 years, what is her age?

36. Pattern Predictor 8

Look at the pattern for the first four stages. For later stages, make a drawing if it helps you answer the questions.

stage 1

stage 2

stage 3

stage 4

1. How many hearts are there at stage 5?

2. How many hearts are there at stage 6?

3. How many hearts are there at stage 7 and stage 8? Complete the table to show the number of hearts for stages 1 through 8.

stage	1	2	3	4	5	6	7	8
number of hearts								

4. How many hearts are there at stage 11?

5. How many hearts are there at stage 14?

36. Pattern Predictor 8 (continued)

6. Look at the pattern and then draw stage 4. For later stages, make a drawing if it helps you answer the questions.

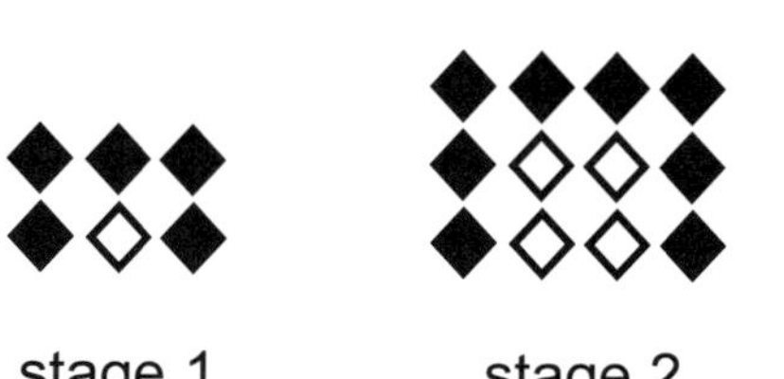

stage 1 stage 2 stage 3 stage 4

7. How many unshaded diamonds ◇ are there at stage 4?

8. How many shaded diamonds ◆ are there at stage 4?

9. How many unshaded diamonds are there at stage 5? How many shaded diamonds are there at stage 5? What is the total number of diamonds at stage 5?

- unshaded: ______
- shaded: ______
- total: ______

10. Complete the table to show the number of diamonds for stages 1 through 7.

stage	1	2	3	4	5	6	7
number of unshaded diamonds	1						
number of shaded diamonds	5						
total number of diamonds	6						

11. What is the total number of diamonds at stage 10? How many of these diamonds are unshaded? How many of them are shaded?

- unshaded: ______
- shaded: ______
- total: ______

37. Equality Explorer 8

1. If [square] = 5, then [three squares] = ____ .

2. If [circle] = 36, then [quarter circle] = ____ .

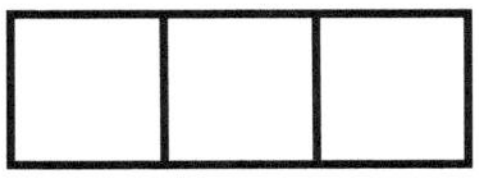

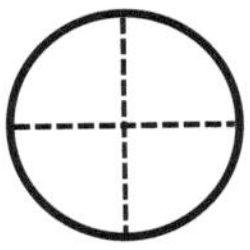

3. If [square and triangle] = 40, then [square] = ____ , [triangle] = ____ .

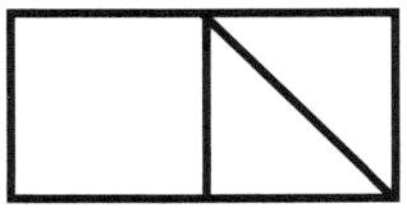

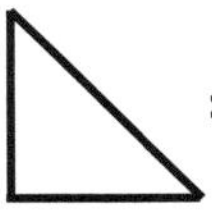

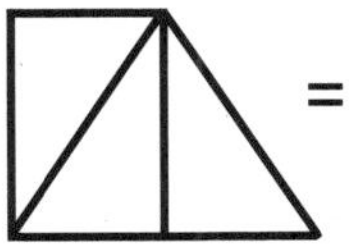

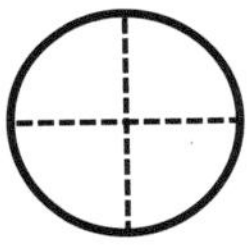

4. If [rectangle] = 16, then [rectangle and triangle] = ____ .

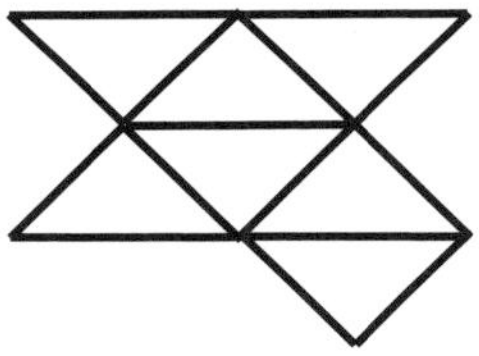

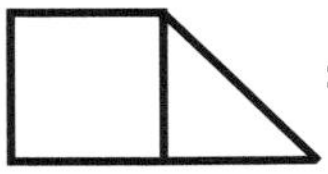

5. If [circle] = 16, then [three-quarter circle] = ____ .

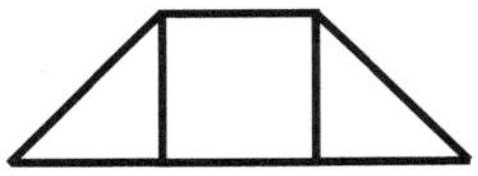

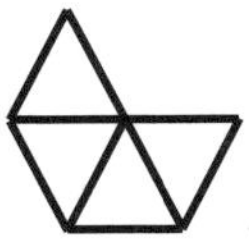

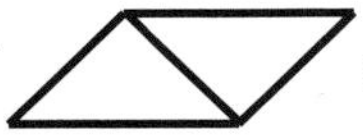

6. If [trapezoid] = 21, then [figure] = ____ .

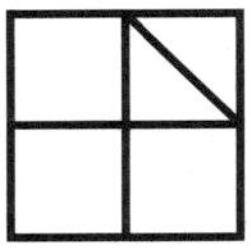

7. If [square and triangle] = 15, then [trapezoid] = ____ .

8. If [hexagon] = 12, then [figure] = ____ .

9. If [parallelogram] = 22, then [trapezoid] = ____ .

10. If [square] = 24, then [triangle] = ____ .

38. Sequence Sleuth 8

The bold lines divide the 4 x 4 square into four 2 x 2 squares. Fill in the grid so that every row, column, and 2 x 2 square contains the 4 shapes above the grid.

1.

2.

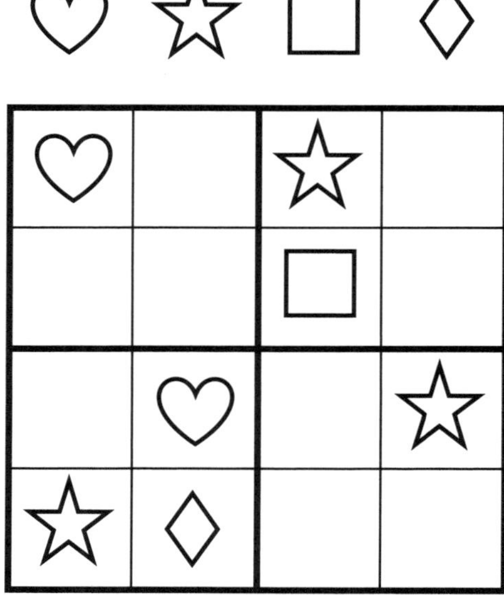

3.

4.

39. Number Ninja 8

Fill in the empty boxes to make the arithmetic work out correctly.

1.

$$\begin{array}{r} \square\,7 \\ +\ 5\,\square \\ \hline 8\,3 \end{array}$$

2.

$$\begin{array}{r} 4\,\square \\ -\ \square\,8 \\ \hline 2\,5 \end{array}$$

3.

$$\begin{array}{r} 2\,\square \\ \times\ \ \ 3 \\ \hline 7\,8 \end{array}$$

4.

$$\begin{array}{r} 6\,\square \\ +\ \square\,8 \\ \hline 1\,0\,0 \end{array}$$

5.

$$\begin{array}{r} \square\,2\,\square \\ -\ \square\,3 \\ \hline 2\,7\,5 \end{array}$$

6.

$$\begin{array}{r} 2\,\square\,3 \\ +\ \square\,9\,\square \\ \hline 9\,4\,0 \end{array}$$

7.

$$\begin{array}{r} \square\,7 \\ \times\ \ \ 4 \\ \hline 1\,4\,8 \end{array}$$

8.

$$\begin{array}{r} \square\,6\,\square \\ +\ 3\,\square\,7 \\ \hline 9\,5\,2 \end{array}$$

9.

$$\begin{array}{r} 8\,\square\,4 \\ -\ \square\,4\,\square \\ \hline 5\,4\,8 \end{array}$$

10.

$$\begin{array}{r} \square\,8\,\square \\ \times\ \ \ \ \ 4 \\ \hline 1\,1\,3\,2 \end{array}$$

11.

$$\begin{array}{r} \square\,2\,\square \\ +\ 7\,\square\,9 \\ \hline 1\,6\,9\,7 \end{array}$$

12.

$$\begin{array}{r} 3\,\square\,2 \\ -\ \square\,8\,\square \\ \hline 5\,5 \end{array}$$

40. Function Finder 8

Complete the table and state the function rule. The first two are done as examples.

1. RULE: ***ADD 4***

in	6	17	30	53	75	***92***	100
out	10	21	34	57	***79***	96	104

2. RULE: ***MULTIPLY BY 2***

in	1	5	12	25	30	***44***	133
out	2	10	24	50	***60***	88	266

3. RULE: ____________________

in	2	5	8	11	20		100
out	6	15	24	33		120	300

4. RULE: ____________________

in	25	40	88	100	143		270
out	36	51	99	111		215	281

5. RULE: ____________________

in	30	48	67	100	149		207
out	23	41	60	93		174	200

6. RULE: ____________________

in	5	15	40	100	250		500
out	1	3	8	20		60	100

7. RULE: ____________________

in	30	42	67	81	93		97
out	33	45	70	84		111	100

8. RULE: ____________________

in	1	4	7	12	19		49
out	10	40	70	120		280	490

9. RULE: ____________________

in	6	22	40	66	84		100
out	3	11	20	33		46	50

10. RULE: ____________________

in	16	27	59	90	148		395
out	11	22	54	85		206	390

Hints

1. Pattern Predictor 1 (p. 1)

- *Hint for questions 1-6*: Each row of circles ○○● has 2 unshaded circles and 1 shaded circle. Stage 5 has 5 rows of circles, for a total of 10 unshaded circles and 5 shaded circles. Stage 6 has 6 rows of circles, for a total of 12 unshaded circles and 6 shaded circles. Continue the pattern to find later stages. For example, stage 10 has 10 rows of circles, for a total of 20 unshaded circles and 10 shaded circles.
- *Hint for questions 7-12*: Increasing the stage number by 1 adds 2 unshaded circles and 2 shaded circles. Stage 3 has 6 unshaded circles and 7 shaded circles, for a total of 13 circles. Stage 4 has 8 unshaded circles and 9 shaded circles, for a total of 17 circles. Stage 5 has 10 unshaded circles and 11 shaded circles, for a total of 21 circles. Keep adding 2 unshaded circles and 2 shaded circles to get later stages.

2. Equality Explorer 1 (p. 3)

- *Hint for question 1*: Two triangles are worth 18, so 1 triangle is worth 9. The diamond is worth 13 since 13 + 7 = 20.
- *Hint for question 2*: Three squares are worth 24, so 1 square is worth 8. Use this result in the first equation: 8 + 5-pointed star = 19, so the 5-pointed star is worth 11.
- *Hint for question 4*: Two clouds + 15 = 25. So 2 clouds must be worth 10, which means 1 cloud is worth 5. Use this result in the second equation: 2 pentagons + 5 = 11. So 2 pentagons are worth 6, which means 1 pentagon is worth 3.
- *Hint for question 5*: The 6-pointed star is worth 7, since in the first equation 7 + 10 + 7 = 24.

3. Sequence Sleuth 1 (p. 4)

- *Hint for all questions*: Later stages can be found by continuing the repeating pattern. For example, in question 1 the pattern that repeats is: lightning bolt (L), cloud (C), cloud (C), or LCC. So the sequence is LCCLCCLCCLCCLCCLCC… So the 7th shape is lightning bolt (L), the 8th shape is cloud (C), the 10th shape is lightning bolt (L), and so on.

4. Number Ninja 1 (p. 5)

- *Hint for question 1*: For the top row, find pairs of numbers that multiply to 6: 1 x 6 = 6 and 2 x 3 = 6. For the bottom row, find pairs of numbers that multiply to 20. You have the right answer when the multiplications also work out for the columns. Two examples are shown where the rows work out. On the left, the columns do not work since 1 x 10 ≠ 8 and 6 x 2 ≠ 15. On the right, the columns do work since 2 x 4 = 8 and 3 x 5 = 15.

NO

1	**6**	6
10	**2**	20
8	15	

YES

2	**3**	6
4	**5**	20
8	15	

- *Hint for remaining questions*: All questions can be handled like the hint for question 1.

5. Function Finder 1 (p. 6)

- *Hint for question 1*: For the examples: 6 + 7 = 13, 11 + 14 = 25, 2 + 7 = 9, and so on.
- *Hint for question 2*: For the examples: 6 x 9 = 54, 7 x 4 = 28, 2 x 5 = 10, and so on.
- *Hint for question 3*: For the examples: 33 – 12 = 21, 16 – 11 = 5, 100 – 30 = 70, and so on.

6. Pattern Predictor 2 (p. 7)

- *Hint for questions 1-6*: Stage 4 has 6 branches, each containing 4 circles: 6 x 4 = 24 circles. Stage 5 has 6 branches, each containing 5 circles: 6 x 5 = 30 circles. Stage 6 has 6 branches, each containing 6 circles: 6 x 6 = 36 circles. Stage 7 has 6 branches, each containing 7 circles: 6 x 7 = 42 circles. Continue the pattern to find later stages.
- *Hint for questions 7 and 8*: Each stage has 6 branches of circles. For question 7, 6 times what number equals 54? That number equals 54 ÷ 6. For question 8, 6 times what number equals 78? That number equals 78 ÷ 6.

- *Hint for questions 9-13*: Stage 1 has 1 diamond. Stage 2 has 1 + 2 = 3 diamonds. Stage 3 has 1 + 2 + 3 = 6 diamonds. Stage 4 has 1 + 2 + 3 + 4 = 10 diamonds. Stage 5 has 1 + 2 + 3 + 4 + 5 = 15 diamonds. Stage 6 has 1 + 2 + 3 + 4 + 5 + 6 = 21 diamonds. Continue the pattern to find later stages.

7. **Equality Explorer 2** (p. 9)
   - *Hint for question 1*: When you subtract 5 from the heart in the first equation you get 11. The heart must be worth 16, since 16 – 5 = 11. Using heart = 16 in the second equation gives 16 + 2 pentagons = 30, which means 2 pentagons are worth 14. So 1 pentagon = 7.
   - *Hint for question 3*: The star is worth 12 since 12 + 12 – 4 = 20 in the second equation.
   - *Hint for question 5*: Start with the first equation: the triangle is worth 9, since 20 – 9 = 11. Using triangle = 9 in the second equation gives 2 lightning bolts + 9 = 19, which means 2 lightning bolts are worth 10. So 1 lightning bolt = 5.

8. **Sequence Sleuth 2** (p. 10)
   - *Hint for question 1*: Start with 7 and keep adding 4.
   - *Hint for question 2*: Start with 98 and keep subtracting 6.
   - *Hint for question 4*: Start with 2 and keep adding 13.
   - *Hint for question 6*: Start with 14 on Monday and keep adding 3: 17 on Tuesday, 20 on Wednesday, 23 on Thursday, 26 on Friday, and so on.

9. **Number Ninja 2** (p. 11)
   - *Hint for question 1*: 18 + 12 = 30 (sum of 2 hearts), 1 + 29 = 30 (sum of 2 clouds), 7 + 23 = 30 (sum of two squares), 15 + 15 = 30 (sum of 2 circles).
   - *Hint for question 2*: What is the sum of the 2 hearts (22 + 3)? What is the sum of the 2 clouds (8 + 17)? What is the sum of the 2 squares (24 + 1)? What is the sum of the 2 circles (20 + 5)?
   - *Hint for question 3*: What is the product of the 2 hearts (3 x 8)? What is the product of the 2 clouds (12 x 2)?
   - *Hint for question 5*: What is the difference between the 2 hearts (88 – 38)? What is the difference between the 2 clouds (64 – 14)?

10. **Function Finder 2** (p. 12)
    - *Hint for question 1*: For the examples: 3 + 1 + 10 = 14, 5 + 10 + 30 = 45, and so on.
    - *Hint for question 2*: For the examples: 2 x 5 x 7 = 70, 3 x 3 x 5 = 45, and so on.
    - *Hint for question 3*: For the examples: 10 + 10 – 3 = 17, 19 + 21 – 2 = 38, and so on.

11. **Pattern Predictor 3** (p. 13)
    - *Hint for questions 1-6*: Stage 4 has 4 rows of 5 triangles: 4 x 5 = 20 triangles. Stage 5 has 5 rows of 6 triangles: 5 x 6 = 30 triangles. Stage 6 has 6 rows of 7 triangles: 6 x 7 = 42 triangles. Continue the pattern to find later stages. Stage 10 has 10 rows of 11 triangles: 10 x 11 = 110 triangles.
    - *Hint for questions 7-12*: Stage 4 has 5 rows of 4 circles: 5 x 4 = 20 circles. Stage 5 has 5 rows of 5 circles: 5 x 5 = 25 circles. Stage 6 has 5 rows of 6 circles: 5 x 6 = 30 circles. Continue the pattern to find later stages. Stage 10 has 5 rows of 10 circles: 5 x 10 = 50 circles.
    - *Hint for questions 13 and 14*: Each stage has 5 rows of circles. For question 13, 5 times what number equals 40? That number equals 40 ÷ 5. For question 14, 5 times what number equals 75? That number equals 75 ÷ 5.

12. **Equality Explorer 3** (p. 15)
    - *Hint for all questions*: Use guess-and-check: explore, plug numbers into the squares, and see what you get. Remember to use each number only once.

13. Sequence Sleuth 3 (p. 16)
- *Hint for question 1*: Keep adding 25 minutes to go from one time to the next.
- *Hint for question 2*: Keep adding 40 minutes to go from one time to the next.
- *Hint for question 3*: Keep adding 1 hour, 15 minutes to go from one time to the next.

14. Number Ninja 3 (p. 17)
- *Hint for question 1*: The top circle is 5 x 9 = 45, the bottom circle is 5 + 9 = 14.
- *Hint for question 3*: To get the number in the empty square on the right: 6 times what number equals 42? Once you get that the right square's number equals 7, add the two squares to get the bottom circle: 6 + 7 = 13.
- *Hint for question 5*: There are two pairs of numbers that multiply to 15 (the top circle): 1 x 15 = 15 and 3 x 5 = 15. Which pair of numbers add up to 8 (the bottom circle)?
- *Hint for question 20*: Remember that 1 x 14 = 14.

15. Function Finder 3 (p. 18)
- *Hint for question 1*: The output is 6 more than the input 47: 47 + 6 = 53.
- *Hint for question 2*: The input is 6 less than the output 80: 80 – 6 = 74.
- *Hint for question 3b*: The output is 3 times the input. If the input is 7, the output is 3 x 7 = 21. If the output is 45, the input is 15 since 3 x 15 = 45.

16. Pattern Predictor 4 (p. 19)
- *Hint for questions 1-6*: Increasing the stage number by 1 adds 2 toothpicks and 1 gumdrop. Stage 4 has 9 toothpicks and 6 gumdrops. Stage 5 has 11 toothpicks and 7 gumdrops. Stage 6 has 13 toothpicks and 8 gumdrops. Keep adding 2 toothpicks and 1 gumdrop to get later stages.
- *Hint for questions 7-12*: Stage 4 has 3 branches of 4 triangles each plus 6 triangles in the middle: 3 x 4 + 6 = 12 + 6 = 18 triangles. Stage 5 has 3 branches of 5 triangles each plus 6 triangles in the middle: 3 x 5 + 6 = 15 + 6 = 21 triangles. Stage 6 has 3 branches of 6 triangles each plus 6 triangles in the middle: 3 x 6 + 6 = 18 + 6 = 24 triangles. Continue the pattern to find later stages. For example, stage 12 has 3 branches of 12 triangles each plus 6 triangles in the middle: 3 x 12 + 6 = 36 + 6 = 42 triangles.

17. Equality Explorer 4 (p. 21)
- *Hint for question 1*: The left column tells us triangle + triangle = 40, so 1 triangle = 20. The top row tells us triangle + circle = 39, so 20 + circle = 39, which means circle = 19.
- *Hint for question 2*: The bottom row tells us heart + heart = 8, so 1 heart = 4. The left column tells us 2 diamonds + heart = 34, so 2 diamonds + 4 = 34, which means 2 diamonds = 30. So 1 diamond = 15.

18. Sequence Sleuth 4 (p. 22)
- *Hint for question 7*: Keep subtracting 10 to go from one term to the next.
- *Hint for question 9*: Keep multiplying by 2 to go from one term to the next.
- *Hint for question 11*: Keep dividing by 2 to go from one term to the next.

19. Number Ninja 4 (p. 23)
- *Hint 1 for all questions*: Keep searching for rows, columns, and diagonals where you know 2 of the 3 numbers. You can use the two known numbers to find the missing third number. For example, in question 1 the middle number in the top row is 2 since 9 + 2 + 7 = 18.
- *Hint 2 for all questions*: Remember that the numbers in the diagonals must also add up to the indicated sum. For example, in question 1 the middle square is 6 since 9 + 6 + 3 = 18.
- *Hint 3 for all questions*: Remember that there are two diagonals in each question. For example, in question 1 the lower left square is 5 since the middle square is 6 (see Hint 2) and 5 + 6 + 7 = 18.

20. Function Finder 4 (p. 24)

- *Hint for question 1*: Start with the smallest number in the upper left corner and then keep adding 1 in a clockwise direction. For 1a: 60 is in the top left, 61 is in the top right, 62 is in the lower right, and 63 is in the lower left.
- *Hint for question 2*: Start with the smallest number in the upper left corner and then keep adding 3 in a clockwise direction. For 2a: 22 is in the top left, 25 is in the top right, 28 is in the lower right, and 31 is in the lower left.

21. Pattern Predictor 5 (p. 25)

- *Hint for questions 1-6*: Increasing the stage number by 1 adds 3 toothpicks and 2 gumdrops. Stage 4 has 13 toothpicks and 10 gumdrops. Stage 5 has 16 toothpicks and 12 gumdrops. Stage 6 has 19 toothpicks and 14 gumdrops. Keep adding 3 toothpicks and 2 gumdrops to get later stages.
- *Hint for questions 7-12*: Stage 4 has 4 rows of 4 stars each: 4 x 4 = 16 stars. Stage 5 has 5 rows of 5 stars each: 5 x 5 = 25 stars. Stage 6 has 6 rows of 6 stars each: 6 x 6 = 36 stars. Continue the pattern to find later stages. For example, stage 10 has 10 rows of 10 stars each: 10 x 10 = 100 stars.

22. Equality Explorer 5 (p. 27)

- *Hint for question 2*: For the second equation, you want to find two numbers that multiply to 30: 1 x 30 = 30, 2 x 15 = 30, 3 x 10 = 30, 5 x 6 = 30. Which pair of numbers also satisfies the first equation? It is 6 and 5 since 6 – 5 = 1.
- *Hint for question 4*: For the second equation, you want to find two different whole numbers that add up to 10: 9 + 1 = 10, 8 + 2 = 10, 7 + 3 = 10, 6 + 4 = 10. Which pair of numbers also satisfies the first equation? It is 8 and 2 since 8 ÷ 2 = 4.
- *Hint for question 5*: The triangle is worth 12 since 12 + 12 + 6 = 30 (first equation). Use that triangle = 12 in the second equation: 2 lightning bolts – 12 = 8, so 2 lightning bolts = 20, which means 1 lightning bolt = 10.

23. Sequence Sleuth 5 (p. 28)

- *Hint 1 for all questions*: Search for a number pattern in each question. In question 1, you keep adding 3: 3, 6, 9, 12, 15, 18, 21, 24, 27, and so on. In question 2, you keep adding 4: 4, 8, 12, 16, 20, 24, 28, 32, 36, and so on. In question 3, you keep adding 5: 1, 6, 11, 16, 21, 26, 31, 36, 41, 46, and so on.
- *Hint 2 for all questions*: In addition to number patterns, also look for geometric patterns formed by the circles.

24. Number Ninja 5 (p. 29)

- *Hint for all questions*: You can apply the rule to use higher numbers to solve for lower missing numbers. For example, in question 2 since 18 + 7 = 25 the missing number equals 7.

From question 2:

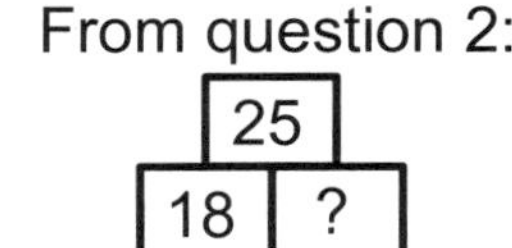

25. Function Finder 5 (p. 30)

- *Hint for question 2a*: When you input 2, the output is 2 x 5 = 10. When you input 6, the output is 6 x 5 = 30. When you input 9, the output is 9 x 5 = 45.
- *Hint for question 3a*: The function rule is to multiply the number of gallons by 4 to get the number of quarts: 3 gallons give you 3 x 4 = 12 quarts, 5 gallons give you 5 x 4 = 20 quarts, and so on.
- *Hint for question 3b*: Using the rule from 3a: 15 gallons give you 15 x 4 = 60 quarts.
- *Hint for question 3c*: Using the rule from 3a: 10 gallons give you 10 x 4 = 40 quarts.
- *Hint for question 4*: The function rule is to multiply the number of feet by 12 to get the number of inches: 2 feet are worth 2 x 12 = 24 inches, 3 feet are worth 3 x 12 = 36 inches, and so on.

26. Pattern Predictor 6 (p. 31)

- *Hint for questions 1-6*: Increasing the stage number by 1 adds 4 toothpicks and 3 gumdrops. Stage 4 has 17 toothpicks and 14 gumdrops. Stage 5 has 21 toothpicks and 17 gumdrops. Stage 6 has 25 toothpicks and 20 gumdrops. Keep adding 4 toothpicks and 3 gumdrops to get later stages.
- *Hint for questions 7-12*: Stage 5 has 7 rows of 5 circles each: 7 x 5 = 35 circles. Stage 6 has 8 rows of 6 circles each: 8 x 6 = 48 circles. Stage 7 has 9 rows of 7 circles each: 9 x 7 = 63 circles. Continue the pattern to find later stages. For example, stage 11 has 13 rows of 11 circles each: 13 x 11 = 143 circles.

27. Equality Explorer 6 (p. 33)

- *Hint 1 for all questions*: Search for a row or column that has only 1 missing number. You can use the remaining number(s) in that row or column to find the missing number. For example, in question 1 the top left square must be 8 since in the top row 8 + 13 = 21.
- *Hint 2 for all questions*: As you find missing numbers, keep searching for new rows or columns that have only 1 missing number. For example, in question 1 after you determine the top left square is 8 (see Hint 1) you can then determine that the bottom left square must be 7 since 8 + 7 = 15 in the left column.

28. Sequence Sleuth 6 (p. 34)

- *Hint for questions 1-3*: Later stages can be found by continuing the repeating pattern. For example, in question 1 the pattern that repeats is: star (S), star (S), diamond (D), circle (C), or SSDC. So the sequence is SSDCSSDCSSDCSSDCSSDC… So the 9th shape is a star (S) and the 11th shape is a diamond (D).
- *Hint for question 4*: The pattern is growing rather than repeating: 1 A, then 2 Bs, then 3 Cs, then 4 Ds, then 5 Es, then 6 Fs, and so on: ABBCCCDDDDEEEEEFFFFFF…

29. Number Ninja 6 (p. 35)

- *Hint 1 for all questions*: First use triangle sides that have only 1 missing number. You can use the remaining numbers in that side to find the missing number. For example, in question 1 the middle circle on the bottom side must be 4 since 3 + 4 + 2 = 9.
- *Hint 2 for all questions*: There are sides with 2 numbers missing, so be prepared to use guess-and-check when needed: plug in different numbers and keep searching until you get the desired sum.
- *Hint 3 for all questions*: Though not necessary, you can guide your guess-and-check searches using the fact that, for a given triangle, all sides have the same sum. For example, in question 3: since the number 5 is greater than the number 1, the lower left circle must be greater than the top circle.
- *Hint for question 3*: Try 2 in the top circle.
- *Hint for question 4*: Try 6 in the lower right circle.
- *Hint for question 7*: Try 8 in the lower right circle.
- *Hint for question 8*: Try 3 in the top circle.

30. Function Finder 6 (p. 36)

- *Hint for question 2a*: When you input 14, the output is 14 + 10 = 24. When you input 21, the output is 21 + 10 = 31. When you input 29, the output is 29 + 10 = 39.
- *Hint for question 3*: Amanda is 8 years older than Spencer.
- *Hint for question 4*: The selling price of the cake is $5 more than the cost to make the cake.
- *Hint for question 5*: Sammy does 15 less pushups than situps.

31. Pattern Predictor 7 (p. 37)

- *Hint for questions 1-6*: Stage 4 has 4 branches of 4 stars each plus 9 stars in the middle: 4 x 4 + 9 = 16 + 9 = 25 stars. Stage 5 has 4 branches of 5 stars each plus 9 stars in the middle: 4 x 5 + 9 = 20 + 9 = 29 stars. Stage 6 has 4 branches of 6 stars each plus 9 stars in the middle: 4 x 6 + 9 = 24 + 9 = 33 stars. Continue the pattern to find later stages. For example, stage 12 has 4 branches of 12 stars each plus 9 stars in the middle: 4 x 12 + 9 = 48 + 9 = 57 stars.

- *Hint for questions 7-10*: The number of open dots doubles each time the stage number increases by 1: stage 1 has 2 open dots, stage 2 has 4 open dots, stage 3 has 8 open dots, stage 4 has 16 open dots, stage 5 has 32 open dots, stage 6 has 64 open dots, and so on.

32. Equality Explorer 7 (p. 39)

- *Hint for question 2*: The pentagon is 2 since 2 x 2 x 2 = 8.
- *Hint for question 3*: If circle plus half-circle equals 9, then circle = 6 and half-circle = 3.
- *Hint for question 4*: 9 + 1 = 10 and 9 – 1 = 8.

33. Sequence Sleuth 7 (p. 40)

- *Hint for question 1*: Keep subtracting 6 to go from one term to the next.
- *Hint for question 2*: Add 1, then add 2, then add 3, then add 4, then add 5, and so on.
- *Hint for question 3*: Add 4, then add 1, then add 4, then add 1, then add 4, then add 1, and so on.
- *Hint for question 4*: Subtract 8, then subtract 2, then subtract 8, then subtract 2, and so on.
- *Hint for question 5*: Keep multiplying by 2 to go from one term to the next.
- *Hint for question 6*: Subtract 8, then add 3, then subtract 8, then add 3, and so on.

34. Number Ninja 7 (p. 41)

- *Hint for questions 1-10*: Before filling in the blank with the missing number, first do the calculations that are ready to be done. For example: in question 1 first do 9 x 7 = 63 to give the equation 27 + __ = 63, in question 2 first do 60 ÷ 4 = 15 to give the equation 48 – __ = 15.
- *Hint for questions 11-18*: Be prepared to use guess-and-check to explore different possibilities, and remember to use each number only once.

35. Function Finder 7 (p. 42)

- *Hint for question 1a*: Each cheeseburger costs $5: 3 cheeseburgers cost 3 x $5 = $15, 5 cheeseburgers cost 5 x $5 = $25, 8 cheeseburgers cost 8 x $5 = $40, and so on.
- *Hint for question 1b*: Since each cheeseburger costs $5 (see Hint for question 1a), 30 cheeseburgers cost 30 x $5 = $150.
- *Hint for question 1c*: Since each cheeseburger costs $5 (see Hint for question 1a), 12 cheeseburgers cost 12 x $5 = $60.
- *Hint for question 2*: Each class lasts 40 minutes.
- *Hint for question 3*: Each minute of walking burns 4 calories.
- *Hint for question 4*: The teacher has taught 22 fewer years than her age. For example, if the teacher is 50 years old, she has taught for 50 – 22 = 28 years.

36. Pattern Predictor 8 (p. 43)

- *Hint for questions 1-5*: Stage 1 has 6 hearts. Stage 2 has 6 + 4 = 10 hearts. Stage 3 has 6 + 4 + 6 = 16 hearts. Stage 4 has 6 + 4 + 6 + 4 = 20 hearts. Stage 5 has 6 + 4 + 6 + 4 + 6 = 26 hearts. Stage 6 has 6 + 4 + 6 + 4 + 6 + 4 = 30 hearts. Continue the pattern to find later stages. For example, stage 11 has 6 + 4 + 6 + 4 + 6 + 4 + 6 + 4 + 6 + 4 + 6 = 56 hearts.
- *Hint 1 for questions 6-11*: Stage 1 has 1 unshaded diamond. Stage 2 has 2 x 2 = 4 unshaded diamonds. Stage 3 has 3 x 3 = 9 unshaded diamonds. Stage 4 has 4 x 4 = 16 unshaded diamonds. Stage 5 has 5 x 5 = 25 unshaded diamonds. Stage 6 has 6 x 6 = 36 unshaded diamonds. Continue the pattern to find later stages. For example, stage 10 has 10 x 10 = 100 unshaded diamonds.
- *Hint 2 for questions 6-11*: Stage 1 has 5 shaded diamonds, and you keep adding 3 shaded diamonds to go from one stage to the next: stage 2 has 8 shaded diamonds, stage 3 has 11 shaded diamonds, stage 4 has 14 shaded diamonds, stage 5 has 17 shaded diamonds, and so on. Continue the pattern to find later stages.

37. Equality Explorer 8 (p. 45)

- *Hint for question 2*: A circle is worth 36, so a quarter-circle is worth 36 ÷ 4 = 9.
- *Hint for question 3*: Two squares are worth 40, so 1 square is worth 20 and a half-square (a triangle) is worth 10.
- *Hint for question 6*: Three triangles are worth 21, so 1 triangle is worth 7 and 7 triangles are worth 7 x 7 = 49.
- *Hint for question 8*: Six triangles are worth 12, so 1 triangle is worth 2 and 4 triangles are worth 4 x 2 = 8.

38. Sequence Sleuth 8 (p. 46)

- *Hint 1 for all questions*: You can fill in some empty spaces using the fact that each 2 x 2 square contains the 4 shapes above the grid. For example, in question 2 the bottom left 2 x 2 square contains a star, a heart, and a diamond, so the empty space must contain the one remaining shape – a square.
- *Hint 2 for all questions*: Since every row must contain all 4 shapes, no shape can appear twice in a row. Similarly, since every column must contain all 4 shapes, no shape can appear twice in a column.

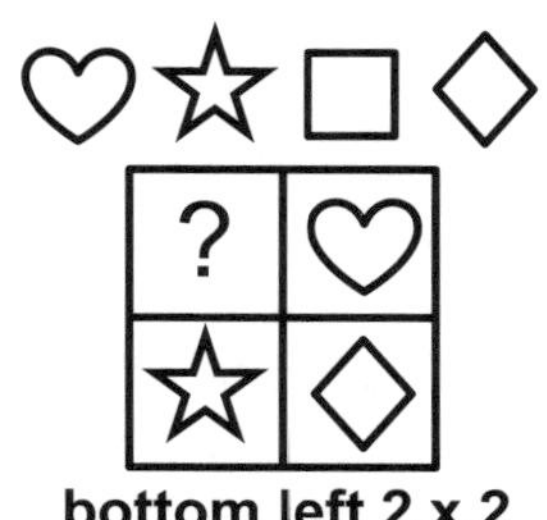

bottom left 2 x 2 square in question 2

39. Number Ninja 8 (p. 47)

- *Hint for all questions*: As you fill in the empty boxes, remember the need for regrouping ("carrying" in addition and "borrowing" in subtraction). For example, in question 1 adding 6 to 7 gives 13, so you must include an extra 1 in the tens column and the empty box in the tens column contains the digit 2.

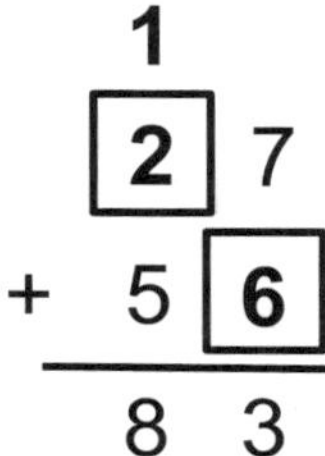

40. Function Finder 8 (p. 48)

- *Hint for all questions*: The function rules could involve any of the four operations: addition, subtraction, multiplication, or division. For a given table, search through several values to determine which operation applies.
- *Hint for question 3*: When you input 2, the output is 2 x 3 = 6. When you input 5, the output is 3 x 5 = 15. When you input 8, the output is 3 x 8 = 24.
- *Hint for question 4*: When you input 25, the output is 25 + 11 = 36. When you input 40, the output is 40 + 11 = 51. When you input 88, the output is 88 + 11 = 99.
- *Hint for question 6*: When you input 5, the output is 5 ÷ 5 = 1. When you input 15, the output is 15 ÷ 5 = 3. When you input 40, the output is 40 ÷ 5 = 8.
- *Hint for question 10*: When you input 16, the output is 16 – 5 = 11. When you input 27, the output is 27 – 5 = 22. When you input 59, the output is 59 – 5 = 54.

Solutions

1. Pattern Predictor 1 (p. 1)

1. 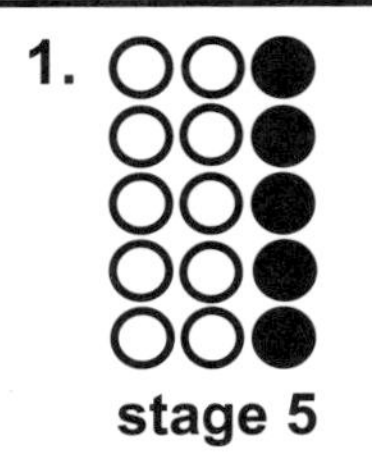
stage 5

2. There are 10 unshaded circles at stage 5.

3. There are 5 shaded circles at stage 5.

Stage 5 has 5 rows of circles.
- Each row has 2 unshaded circles, so there are 5 x 2 = 10 unshaded circles.
- Each row has 1 shaded circle, so there are 5 x 1 = 5 shaded circles.

4. The number of stage 6 circles:
- **total: 18**
- **unshaded: 12**
- **shaded: 6**

stage 6

5. The number of stage 7 circles:
- **total: 21**
- **unshaded: 14**
- **shaded: 7**

stage 7

6. The number of stage 10 circles:
- **total: 30**
- **unshaded: 20**
- **shaded: 10**

stage 10

Stage 10 has 10 rows of circles.
- Each row has 3 circles, so there is a total of 10 x 3 = 30 circles.
- Each row has 2 unshaded circles, so there are 10 x 2 = 20 unshaded circles.
- Each row has 1 shaded circle, so there are 10 x 1 = 10 shaded circles.

7. 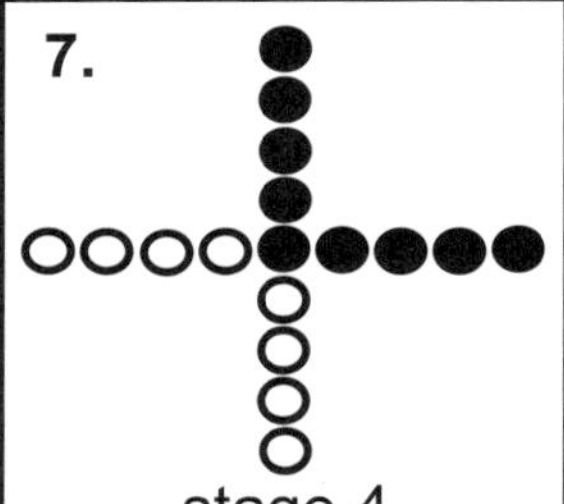
stage 4

8. Stage 4 has 8 unshaded circles.

9. Stage 4 has 9 shaded circles.

10. The number of stage 5 circles:
- **total: 21**
- **unshaded: 10**
- **shaded: 11**

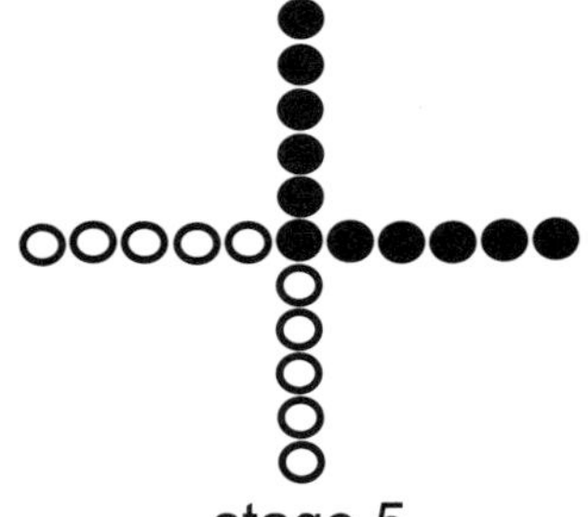
stage 5

11.

stage	1	2	3	4	5	6	7
total number of circles	5	**9**	**13**	**17**	**21**	**25**	**29**
number of unshaded circles	2	**4**	**6**	**8**	**10**	**12**	**14**
number of shaded circles	3	**5**	**7**	**9**	**11**	**13**	**15**

11. (continued)

Each time you increase the stage number by 1, you add 2 unshaded circles and 2 shaded circles (a total of 4 circles, one for each branch). So the total number of circles keeps increasing by 4 (stage 1 has 5 circles, stage 2 has 9 circles, stage 3 has 13 circles, and so on).

12. The number of stage 12 circles:
- **total: 49**
- **unshaded: 24**
- **shaded: 25**

Continue the pattern to get the number of circles at stage 12:

stage	7	8	9	10	11	12
total number of circles	29	33	37	41	45	49
number of unshaded circles	14	16	18	20	22	24
number of shaded circles	15	17	19	21	23	25

2. Equality Explorer 1 (p. 3)

1. ▲ = 9 ◇ = 13

9 + **9** = 18
13 + 7 = 20

2. □ = 8 ★ = 11

8 + **11** = 19
8 + **8** + **8** = 24

3. ▽ = 6 ☾ = 12

6 + **6** = **12**
12 + 7 = 19

4. ☁ = 5 ⬟ = 3

5 + **5** + 15 = 25
3 + **3** + **5** = 11

5. ▰ = 2 ✡ = 7 ✧ = 18

7 + 10 + **7** = 24
2 + **7** = 9
18 + **2** = 20

6. ☺ = 15 ♡ = 4 ϟ = 10

4 + **15** + **10** = 29
15 + **4** + **15** = 34
15 + 13 = 28

3. Sequence Sleuth 1 (p. 4)

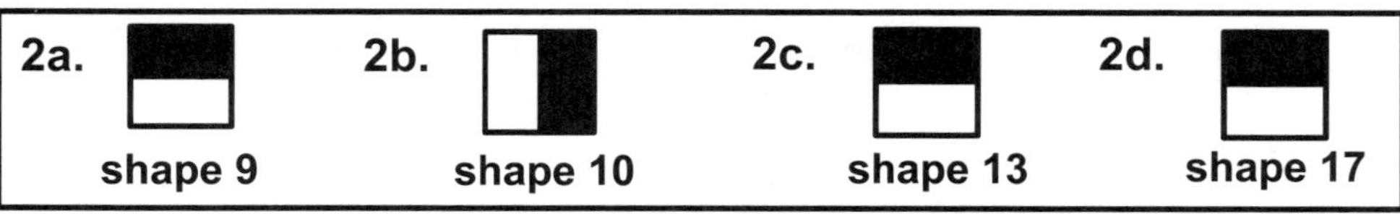

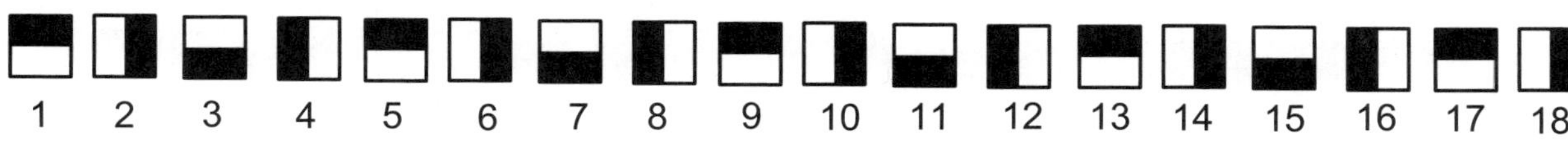

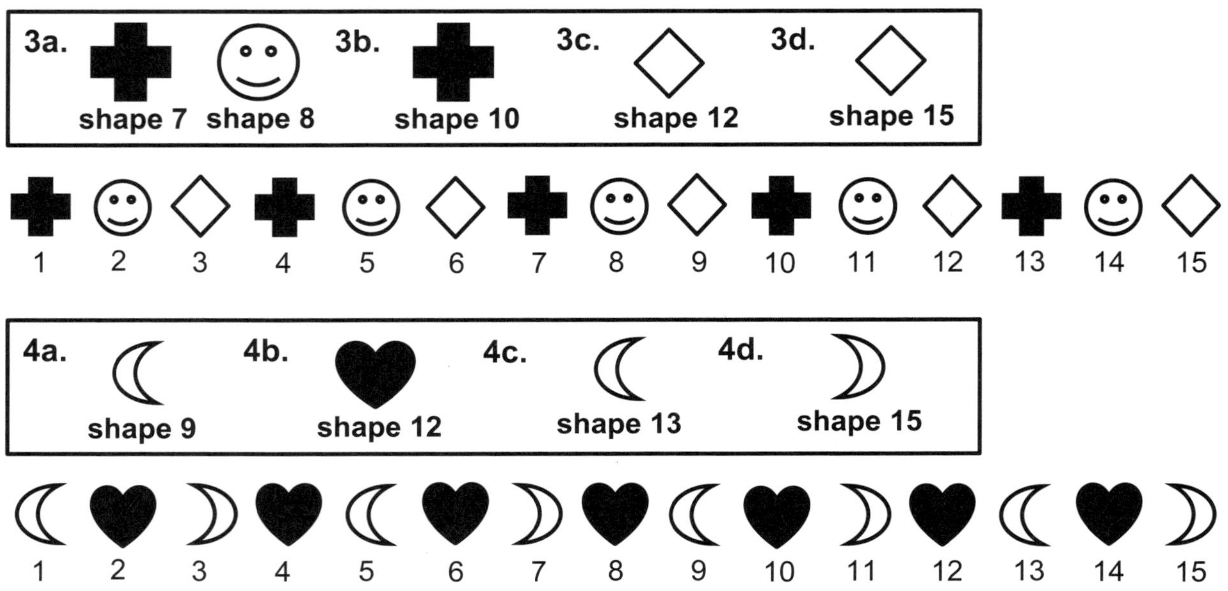

4. Number Ninja 1 (p. 5)

Some questions have more than 1 answer. You need to find only 1 answer.

1.

2	3	6
4	5	20
8	15	

2. Two solutions:

2	7	14
5	4	20
10	28	

1	14	14
10	2	20
10	28	

3.

3	3	9
4	4	16
12	12	

4. Two solutions:

1	5	5
10	1	10
10	5	

5	1	5
2	5	10
10	5	

5.

3	11	33
4	1	4
12	11	

6. Two solutions:

3	9	27
7	6	42
21	54	

1	27	27
21	2	42
21	54	

7. Three solutions:

2	4	8
4	7	28
8	28	

8	1	8
1	28	28
8	28	

4	2	8
2	14	28
8	28	

8.

3	1	3
4	1	4
12	1	

9.

2	11	22
7	5	35
14	55	

10. Two solutions:

2	3	6
1	2	2
2	6	

1	6	6
2	1	2
2	6	

11. Two solutions:

5	6	30
10	3	30
50	18	

10	3	30
5	6	30
50	18	

12. Two solutions:

2	9	18
4	8	32
8	72	

1	18	18
8	4	32
8	72	

13.

5	3	15
10	4	40
50	12	

14. Two solutions:

3	3	9
1	9	9
3	27	

1	9	9
3	3	9
3	27	

15. Two solutions:

5	8	40
6	2	12
30	16	

10	4	40
3	4	12
30	16	

16. Three solutions:

10	10	100
2	2	4
20	20	

5	20	100
4	1	4
20	20	

20	5	100
1	4	4
20	20	

5. Function Finder 1 (p. 6)

1. The top circle is the sum of the two bottom circles. In (a): 3 + 8 = 11.

a. **11** / 3, 8

b. 

c. 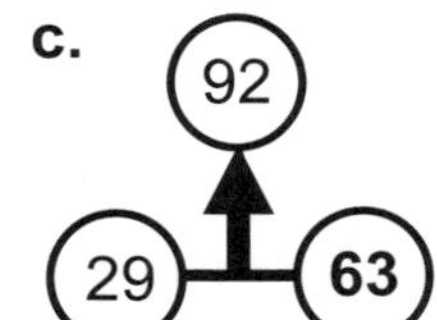

d. 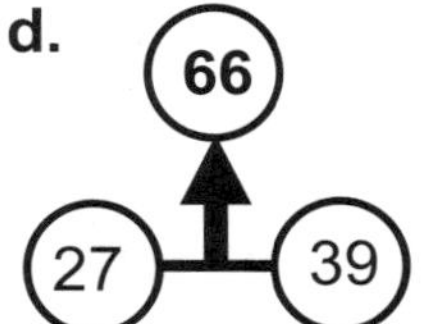

e. 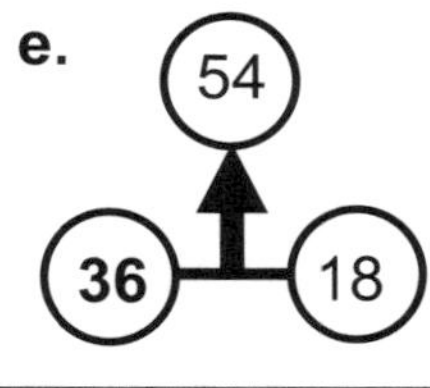

2. The top circle is the product of the two bottom circles. In (a): 8 x 6 = 48.

a. **48** / 8, 6

b. 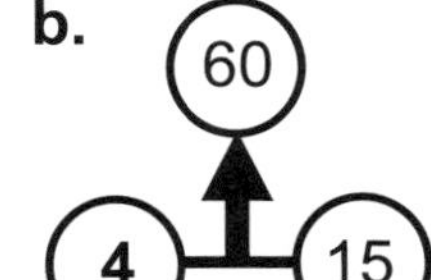

c. 

d. 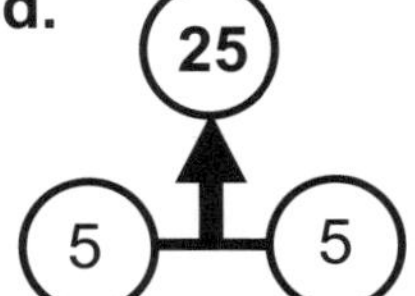

e. 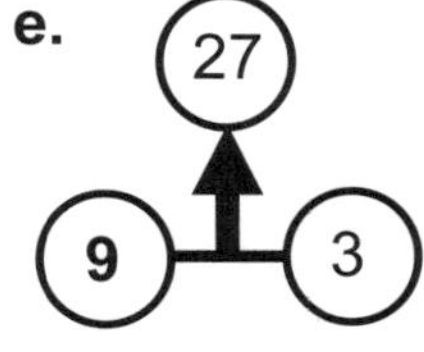

3. The top circle is the difference between the two bottom circles (the left circle minus the right circle). In (a): 11 = 20 – 9.

a. 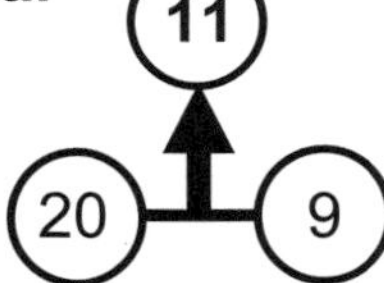

b. 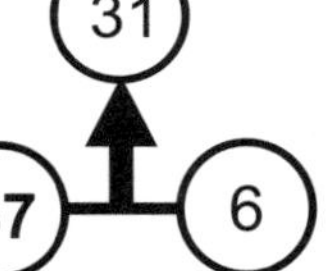

c. 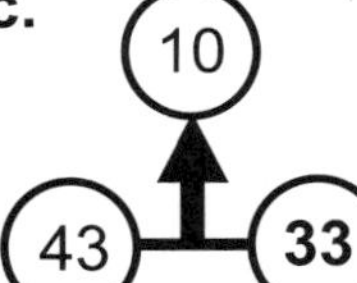

d. 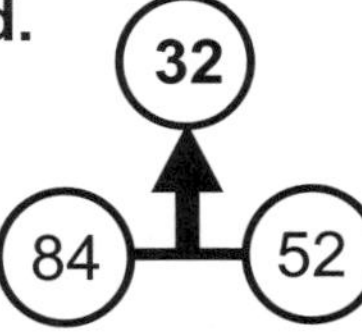

e. 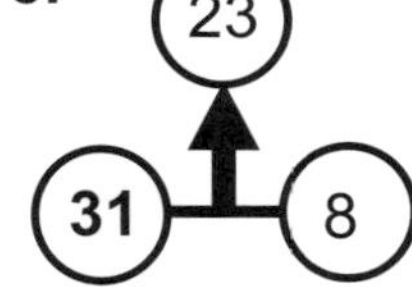

6. Pattern Predictor 2 (p. 7)

1\.

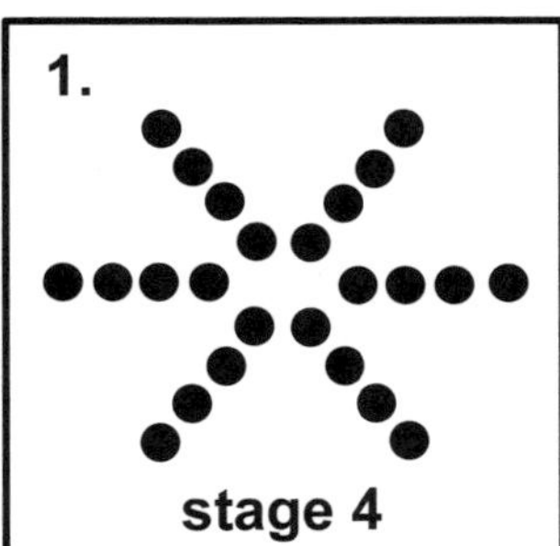

stage 4

2. Stage 4 has 24 circles.

Stage 4 has 6 branches, each with 4 circles, for a total of 6 x 4 = 24 circles.

3. Stage 5 has 30 circles.

Stage 5 has 6 branches, each with 5 circles, for a total of 6 x 5 = 30 circles.

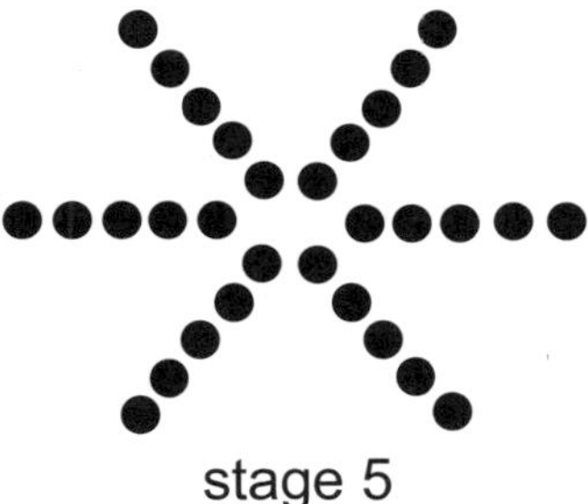

stage 5

4.

stage	1	2	3	4	5	6
number of circles	6	**12**	**18**	**24**	**30**	**36**

5. Stage 7 has 42 circles.

Stage 7 has 6 branches, each with 7 circles, for a total of 6 x 7 = 42 circles.

6. Stage 10 has 60 circles.

Stage 10 has 6 branches, each with 10 circles, for a total of 6 x 10 = 60 circles.

7. Stage 9 has 54 circles.

Stage 9 has 6 branches, each with 9 circles, for a total of 6 x 9 = 54 circles.

8. Stage 13 has 78

Stage 13 has 6 branches, each with 13 circles, for a total of 6 x 13 = 78 circles.

A more complete table helps you understand the answers to questions 7 and 8.

stage	1	2	3	4	5	6	7	8	9	10	11	12	13
number of circles	6	12	18	24	30	36	42	48	54	60	66	72	78

9.

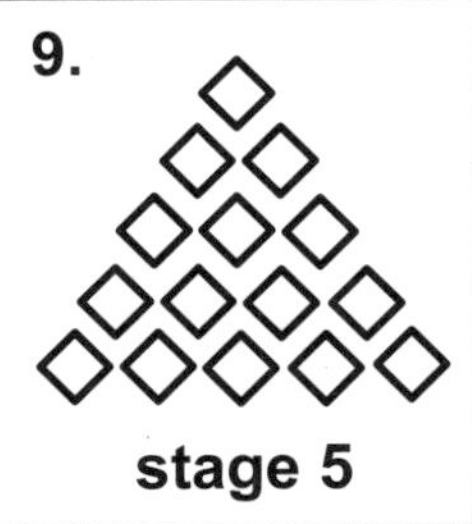

stage 5

10. Stage 5 has 15 diamonds.

11. Stage 6 has 21 diamonds.

Stage 6 has 6 rows of diamonds: the bottom row has 6 diamonds, the second row has 5 diamonds, the third row has 4 diamonds, and so on: 6 + 5 + 4 + 3 + 2 + 1 = 21 diamonds.

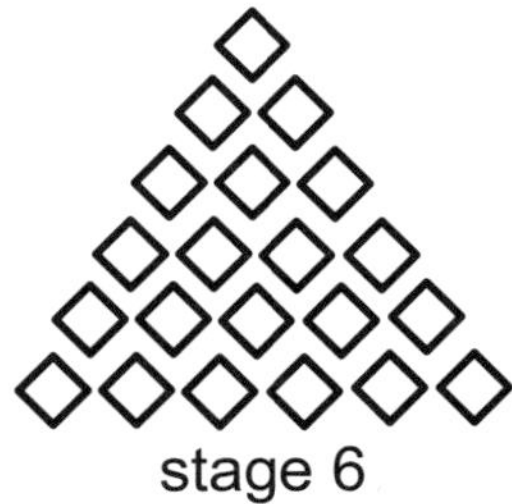

stage 6

12. Stage 7 has 28 diamonds. Stage 8 has 36 diamonds.

stage	number of diamonds
1	1
2	3
3	6
4	10
5	15
6	21
7	28
8	36

+2, +3, +4, +5, +6, +7, +8

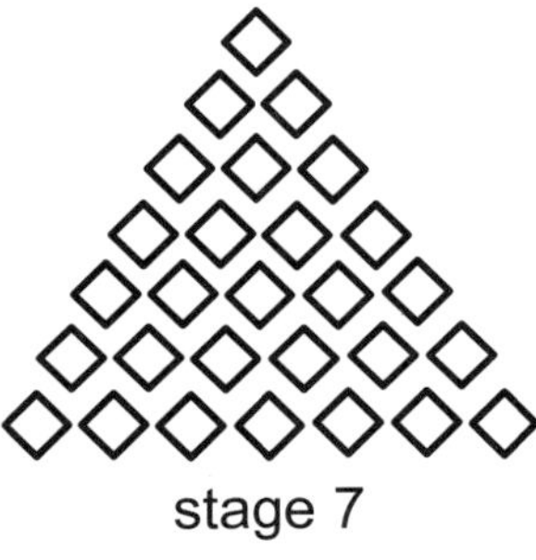

stage 7

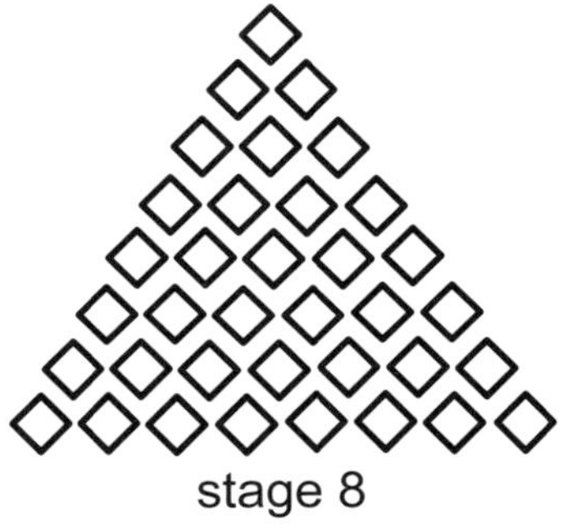

stage 8

Stage 7 has 7 rows of diamonds: 7 + 6 + 5 + 4 + 3 + 2 + 1 = 28 diamonds.
Stage 8 has 8 rows of diamonds: 8+ 7 + 6 + 5 + 4 + 3 + 2 + 1 = 36 diamonds.

13. Stage 2 has 2 more diamonds than stage 1, stage 3 has 3 more diamonds than stage 2, stage 4 has 4 more diamonds than stage 3, and so on.

- **stage 9 has 45 diamonds**
- **stage 10 has 55 diamonds**

Stage 9 has 9 more diamonds than stage 8: 36 + 9 = 45.
Stage 10 has 10 more diamonds than stage 9: 45 + 10 = 55.

7. **Equality Explorer 2** (p. 9)

1. ⬠ **= 7** ♥ **= 16**

16 – 5 = 11
16 + **7** + **7** = 30

2. ☁ **= 13** ⏢ **= 8**

13 – **8** = 5
13 + **13** = 26

3. ★ **= 12** ☾ **= 4**

4 + **4** + **4** = **12**
12 + **12** – 4 = 20

4. ✡ **= 10** ☺ **= 6**

10 + **10** – **6** = 14
6 + **6** – 3 = 9

5. △ **= 9** ⚡ **= 5** ▱ **= 11**

20 – **9** = 11
5 + **5** + **9** = 19
11 – **5** = 6

6. □ **= 1** ◆ **= 20** ✦ **= 15**

20 – **15** = 5
15 – **1** = 14
1 + **1** + 8 = 10

8. **Sequence Sleuth 2** (p. 10)

	1st	2nd	3rd	4th	5th	6th	7th	8th	9th	10th	11th	12th
1.	7	11	15	19	23	**27**	**31**	**35**	**39**	43	**47**	**51**
2.	98	92	86	80	74	**68**	**62**	**56**	**50**	**44**	**38**	32
3.	0	15	**30**	45	**60**	75	90	**105**	**120**	**135**	150	**165**
4.	2	15	28	**41**	54	**67**	**80**	93	**106**	119	**132**	**145**
5.	149	140	131	**122**	113	104	**95**	**86**	77	**68**	**59**	**50**

6. Jamie will have 38 quarters in his piggy bank on Tuesday of next week.

14	17	20	23	26	29	32	35	38
Mon	Tue	Wed	Thu	Fri	Sat	Sun	Mon	Tue

7. Laura will have 36 chocolate bars left to sell on Thursday of next week.

76	72	68	64	60	56	52	48	44	40	36
Mon	Tue	Wed	Thu	Fri	Sat	Sun	Mon	Tue	Wed	Thu

9. Number Ninja 2 (p. 11)

1. The number in the middle circle is 30.

The sum of the numbers opposite each other is 30: 1 + 29 = 30, 18 + 12 = 30, 15 + 15 = 30, 23 + 7 = 30.

2. The number in the middle circle is 25.

The sum of the numbers opposite each other is 25: 8 + 17 = 25, 22 + 3 = 25, 5 + 20 = 25, 1 + 24 = 25.

3. The number in the middle circle is 24.

The product of the numbers opposite each other is 24: 12 x 2 = 24, 3 x 8 = 24, 24 x 1 = 24, 6 x 4 = 24.

4. The number in the middle circle is 36.

The product of the numbers opposite each other is 36: 4 x 9 = 36, 12 x 3 = 36, 6 x 6 = 36, 2 x 18 = 36.

5. The number in the middle circle is 50.

The difference of the numbers opposite each other is 50: 64 – 14 = 50, 88 – 38 = 50, 51 – 1 = 50, 71 – 21 = 50.

6. The number in the middle circle is 13.

The difference of the numbers opposite each other is 13: 15 – 2 = 13, 47 – 34 = 13, 25 – 12 = 13, 29 – 16 = 13.

7. The number in the middle circle is 44.

The sum of the numbers opposite each other is 44: 12 + 32 = 44, 29 + 15 = 44, 21 + 23 = 44, 40 + 4 = 44.

8. The number in the middle circle is 60.

The product of the numbers opposite each other is 60: 10 x 6 = 60, 3 x 20 = 60, 12 x 5 = 60, 1 x 60 = 60.

9. The number in the middle circle is 17.

The difference of the numbers opposite each other is 17: 38 – 21 = 17, 19 – 2 = 17, 24 – 7 = 17, 47 – 30 = 17.

10. Function Finder 2 (p. 12)

1. To get the middle number, add the 3 circled numbers. In (a): 16 + 12 + 5 = 33.

a. 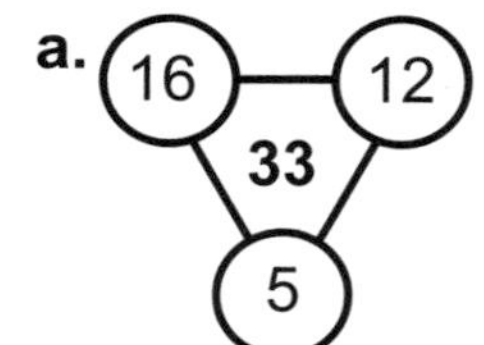

b. 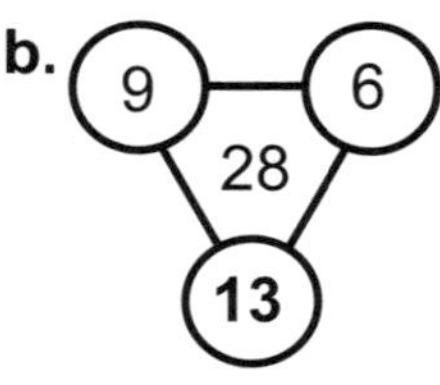

c. 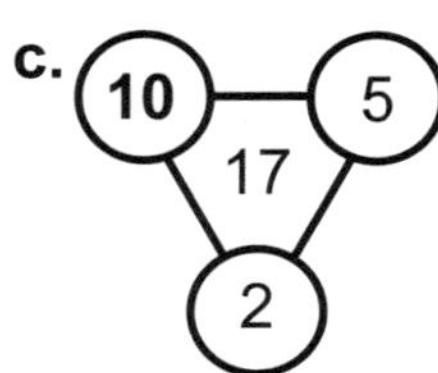

d. 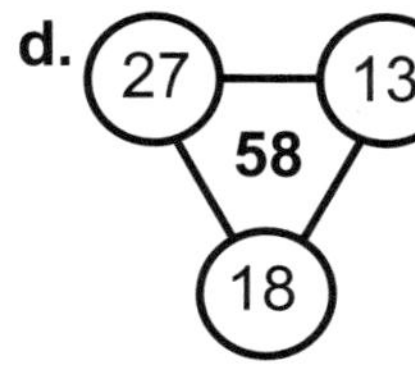

e. 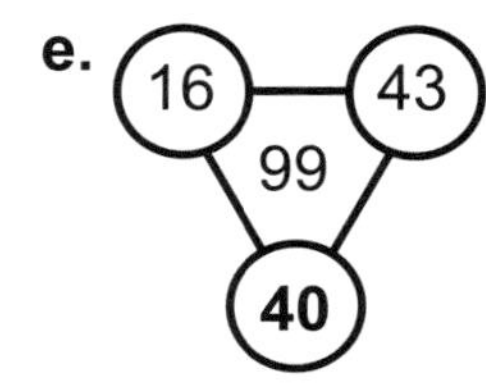

2. To get the middle number, multiply the 3 circled numbers. In (a): 2 x 3 x 6 = 36.

a. 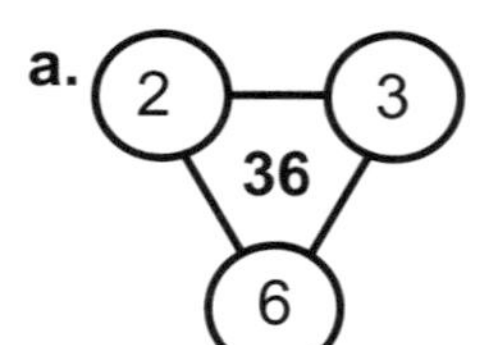

b. 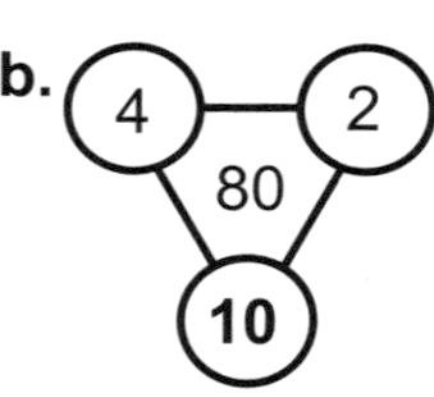

c. 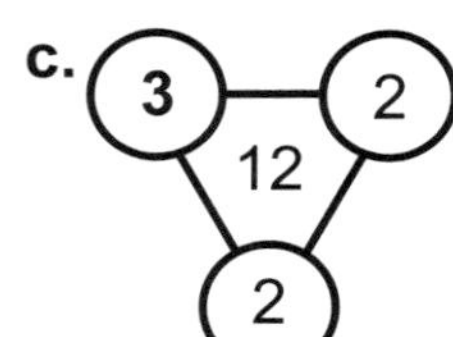

d. 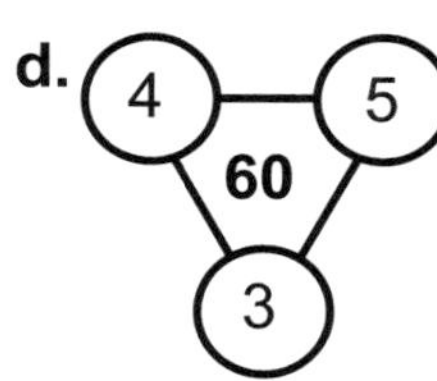

e. 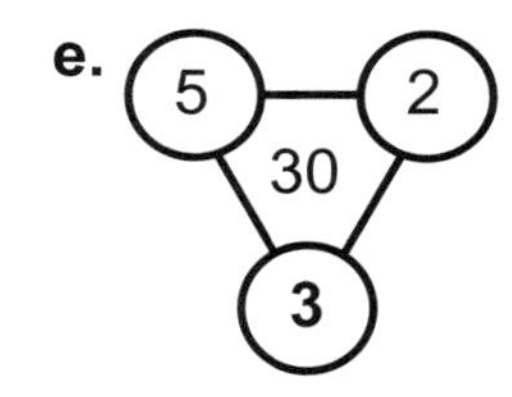

3. To get the middle number, add the top 2 circled numbers and then subtract the bottom circled number. In (a): 15 + 16 – 10 = 21.

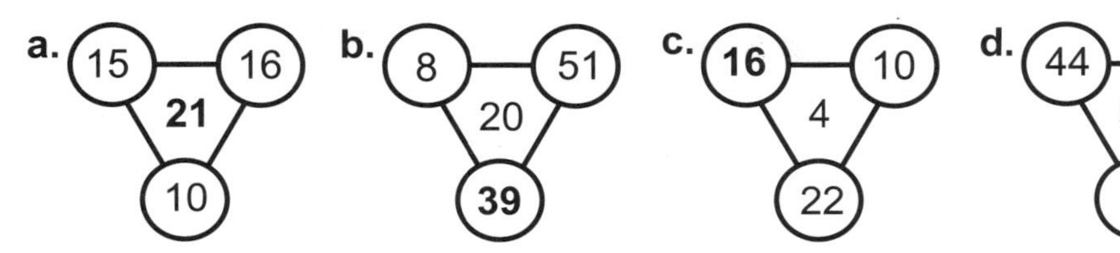

11. Pattern Predictor 3 (p. 13)

1.

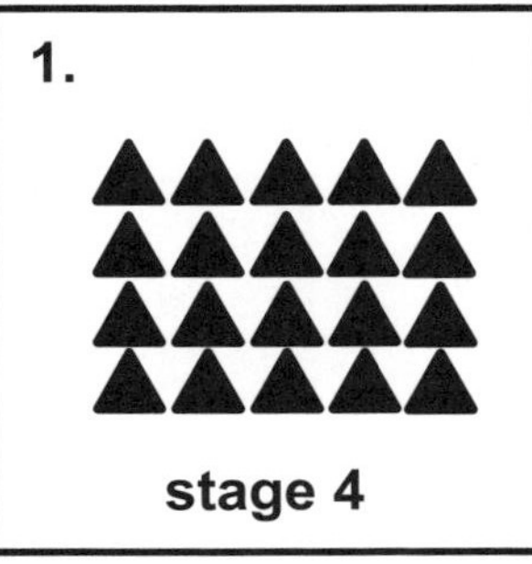

stage 4

2. Stage 4 has 20 triangles.

Stage 4 has 4 rows of 5 triangles each, for a total of 4 x 5 = 20 triangles.

3. Stage 5 has 30 triangles.

Stage 5 has 5 rows of 6 triangles each, for a total of 5 x 6 = 30 triangles.

stage 5

4. Stage 6 has 42 triangles.

Stage 6 has 6 rows of 7 triangles each, for a total of 6 x 7 = 42 triangles.

stage 6

5. Stage 7 has 56 triangles.

Stage 7 has 7 rows of 8 triangles each, for a total of 7 x 8 = 56 triangles.

6. Stage 10 has 110 triangles.

Stage 10 has 10 rows of 11 triangles each, for a total of 10 x 11 = 110 triangles.

7.

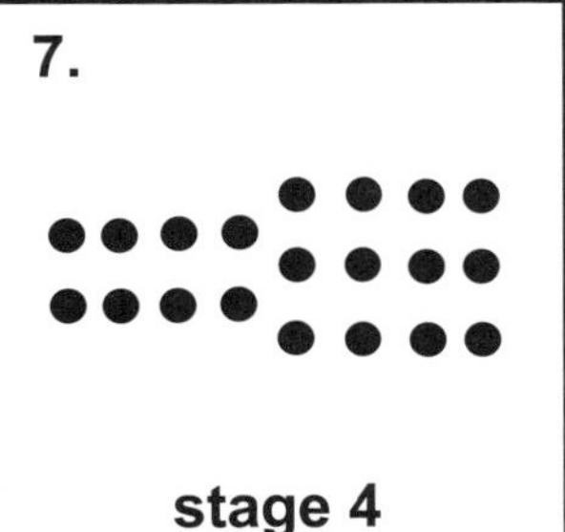

stage 4

8. Stage 4 has 20 circles.

Stage 4 has 5 rows of 4 circles each, for a total of 5 x 4 = 20 circles.

9. Stage 5 has 25 circles.

Stage 5 has 5 rows of 5 circles each, for a total of 5 x 5 = 25 circles.

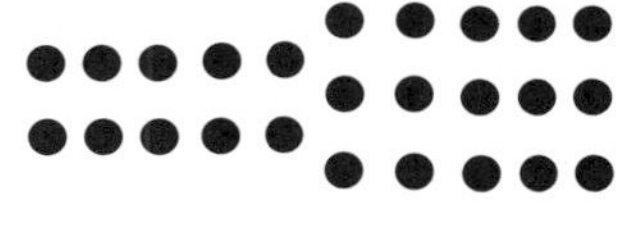

stage 5

10.

stage	1	2	3	4	5	6
number of circles	5	**10**	**15**	**20**	**25**	**30**

11. Stage 7 has 35 circles.

5 rows of 7 circles each = 35 circles.

12. Stage 10 has 50 circles.

5 rows of 10 circles each = 50 circles.

13. Stage 8 has 40 circles.

Stage 8 has 5 rows of 8 circles each, for a total of 5 x 8 = 40 circles.

14. Stage 15 has 75 circles.

Stage 15 has 5 rows of 15 circles each, for a total of 5 x 15 = 75 circles.

A more complete table helps you understand the answers to questions 13 and 14.

stage	1	2	3	4	5	6	7	8	9	10	11	12	13	14	15
number of circles	5	10	15	20	25	30	35	40	45	50	55	60	65	70	75

12. Equality Explorer 3 (p. 15)

1. 10 + 13 = 16 + 7 or 13 + 10 = 16 + 7
2. 6 + 30 = 9 x 4 or 30 + 6 = 9 x 4
3. 4 + 6 = 20 ÷ 2 or 6 + 4 = 20 ÷ 2
4. 3 x 7 = 30 – 9 or 7 x 3 = 30 – 9
5. 6 – 2 = 12 ÷ 3
6. 6 + 14 + 5 = 12 + 13 (can replace 6 + 14 with 14 + 6 or 12 + 13 with 13 + 12)
7. 36 ÷ 6 = 2 + 4 or 36 ÷ 6 = 4 + 2
8. 6 + 8 + 10 = 2 x 12 (or any order of addition with 6 + 8 + 10)
9. 3 + 5 + 8 = 6 + 10 (or any order of addition with 3 + 5 + 8 and 6 + 10)
10. 7 + 8 + 9 = 4 x 6 (or any order with 7 + 8 + 9 and 4 x 6)

13. Sequence Sleuth 3 (p. 16)

1. Last 3 times in sequence:

8:45 am	9:10 am	**9:35 am**

2. Last 2 times in sequence:

8:10 am **8:50 am**

In sequence 1, the times increase by 25 minutes. In sequence 2, the times increase by 40 minutes.

3. Last 3 times in sequence:

2:45 pm	4:00 pm	**5:15 pm**

4. Last 2 times in sequence:

6:00 pm **7:30 pm**

In sequence 3, the times increase by 1 hour and 15 minutes. In sequence 4, the times increase by 1 hour and 30 minutes.

5. Last 3 times in sequence:

7:16 pm	7:34 pm	**7:52 pm**

In sequence 5, the times increase by 18 minutes. In sequence 6, the times increase by 2 hours and 10 minutes.

6. Last 2 times in sequence:

9:30 am **11:40 am**

14. Number Ninja 3 (p. 17)

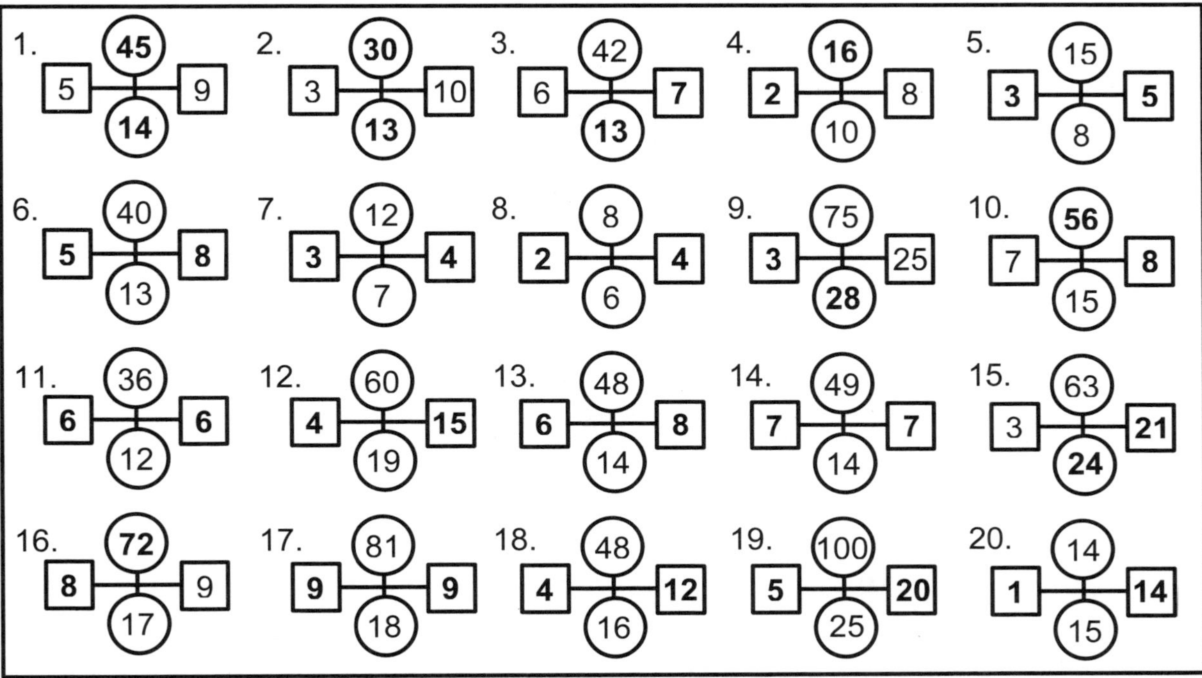

15. Function Finder 3 (p. 18)

1. The output is 53.

The output is 53 since 47 + 6 = 53.

2. The input is 74.

The input is 74 since 74 + 6 = 80.

3a.

in	out
3	15
9	**21**
18	30
32	44
37	**49**
88	100

3b.

in	out
4	12
7	**21**
11	33
15	45
20	**60**
30	90

3c.

in	out
14	5
22	**13**
34	25
50	41
67	**58**
93	84

3d.

in	out
12	3
20	**5**
28	7
48	12
60	**15**
88	22

3e.

in	out
5	22
13	**30**
19	36
31	48
46	**63**
76	93

3f.

in	out
2	12
5	**30**
8	48
10	60
12	**72**
16	96

16. Pattern Predictor 4 (p. 19)

1.

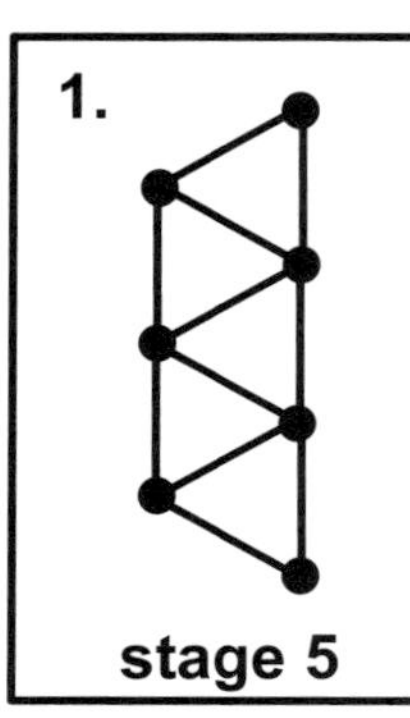

stage 5

2. Stage 5 has 11 toothpicks.

3. Stage 5 has 7 gumdrops.

4. Stage 6 has:

- **13 toothpicks**
- **8 gumdrops**

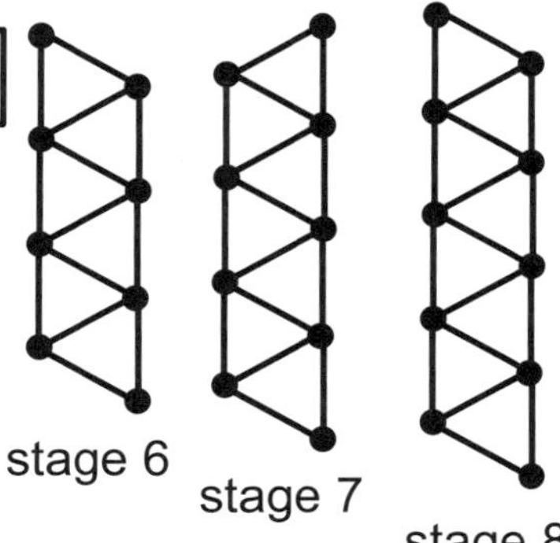

5.

stage	1	2	3	4	5	6	7	8
number of toothpicks	**3**	5	**7**	**9**	**11**	**13**	**15**	**17**
number of gumdrops	**3**	4	**5**	**6**	**7**	**8**	**9**	**10**

When you increase the stage number by 1, the number of toothpicks goes up by 2 and the number of gumdrops goes up by 1. Continue the pattern to find stage 12.

6. Stage 12 has:

- **25 toothpicks**
- **14 gumdrops**

stage	8	9	10	11	12
number of toothpicks	17	19	21	23	25
number of gumdrops	10	11	12	13	14

7.

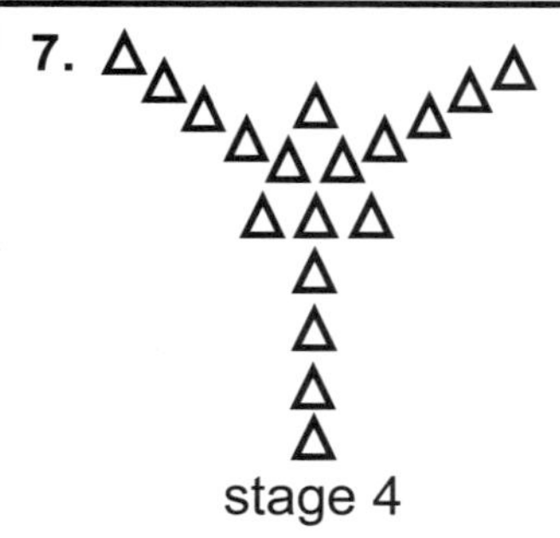

stage 4

8. Stage 4 has 18 triangles.

Stage 4 has 3 branches of 4 triangles each plus 6 triangles in the middle: 3 x 4 + 6 = 12 + 6 = 18.

9. Stage 5 has 21 triangles.

Stage 5 has 3 branches of 5 triangles each plus 6 triangles in the middle: 3 x 5 + 6 = 15 + 6 = 21.

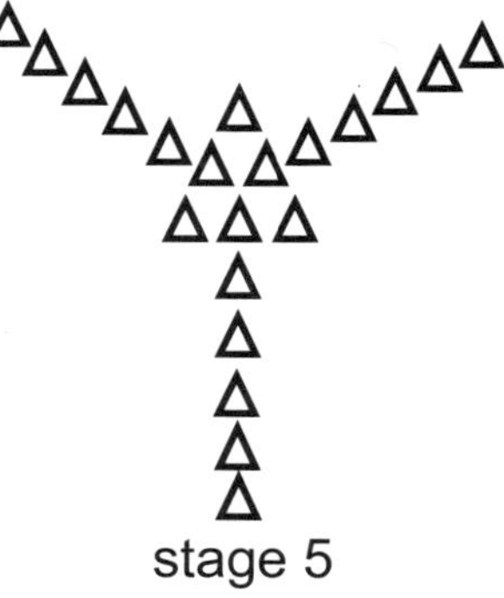

stage 5

10.

stage	1	2	3	4	5	6	7
number of triangles	9	**12**	**15**	**18**	**21**	**24**	**27**

11. Stage 8 has 30 triangles.

12. Stage 12 has 42 triangles.

Continue the pattern to get the number of triangles for stages 8 and 12.

stage	7	8	9	10	11	12
number of triangles	27	30	33	36	39	42

17. Equality Explorer 4 (p. 21)

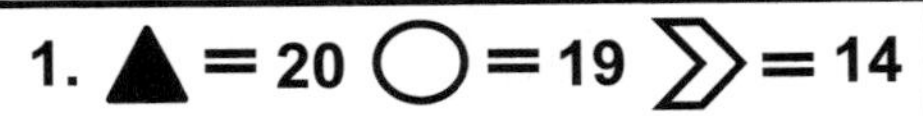

20	**19**	39
20	**14**	34
40	33	

top row: 20 + 19 = 39
bottom row: 20 + 14 = 34
left column: 20 + 20 = 40
right column: 19 + 14 = 33

2. = 7 = 4 = 15 = 11

15	**11**	26
15	**7**	22
4	**4**	8
34	22	

top row: 15 + 11 = 26
middle row: 15 + 7 = 22
bottom row: 4 + 4 = 8
left column: 15 + 15 + 4 = 34
right column: 11 + 7 + 4 = 22

3. = 9 =10 = 5 = 12 = 30

9	**10**	**9**	28
30	**10**	**5**	45
12	**10**	**5**	27
51	30	19	

4. = 3 = 6 = 1 = 13 = 2

13	**6**	**13**	**2**	34
3	**6**	**3**	**3**	15
1	**6**	**1**	**3**	11
2	**6**	**6**	**2**	16
19	24	23	10	

18. Sequence Sleuth 4 (p. 22)

1. 3, 6, 12, 24, 48	**7. starting number: 115**	**rule: subtract 10**
2. 10, 35, 60, 85, 110	**8. starting number: 25**	**rule: add 12**
3. 80, 40, 20, 10, 5	**9. starting number: 15**	**rule: multiply by 2**
4. 99, 92, 85, 78, 71	**10. starting number: 50**	**rule: subtract 4**
5. 1, 3, 9, 27, 81	**11. starting number: 64**	**rule: divide by 2**
6. 32, 40, 48, 56, 64	**12. starting number: 19**	**rule: add 8**

19. Number Ninja 4 (p. 23)

1. sum = 18

9	**2**	7
4	**6**	**8**
5	**10**	3

rows:
9 + 2 + 7 = 18
4 + 6 + 8 = 18
5 + 10 + 3 = 18
columns:
9 + 4 + 5 = 18
2 + 6 + 10 = 18
7 + 8 + 3 = 18
diagonals:
9 + 6 + 3 = 18
5 + 6 + 7 = 18

2. sum = 30

7	**12**	**11**
14	10	**6**
9	**8**	13

3. sum = 21

8	**9**	**4**
3	7	11
10	**5**	**6**

4. sum = 40

19	**4**	**14**	3
5	12	**10**	13
6	**17**	1	**16**
10	7	**15**	**8**

5. sum = 24

10	**4**	**4**	**6**
3	7	9	5
8	6	2	**8**
3	7	**9**	5

6. sum = 70

30	**14**	14	**12**
10	16	**26**	**18**
21	23	**5**	21
9	**17**	25	19

20. Function Finder 4 (p. 24)

1. Start with the smallest number in the top left corner and keep adding 1 as you go around the square in a clockwise direction.

a.

60	61
63	62

b.

25	**26**
28	27

c.

73	**74**
76	75

d.

48	49
51	**50**

e.

67	**68**
70	**69**

2. Start with the smallest number in the top left corner and keep adding 3 as you go around the square in a clockwise direction.

a.

22	**25**
31	28

b.

47	50
56	**53**

c.

38	**41**
47	44

d.

80	**83**
89	**86**

e.

6	9
15	**12**

3. Start with the smallest number in the top left corner and keep adding 7 as you go around the square in a clockwise direction.

a.

12	19
33	26

b.

44	51
65	**58**

c.

36	**43**
57	50

d.

71	78
92	85

e.

65	**72**
86	**79**

21. Pattern Predictor 5 (p. 25)

1.

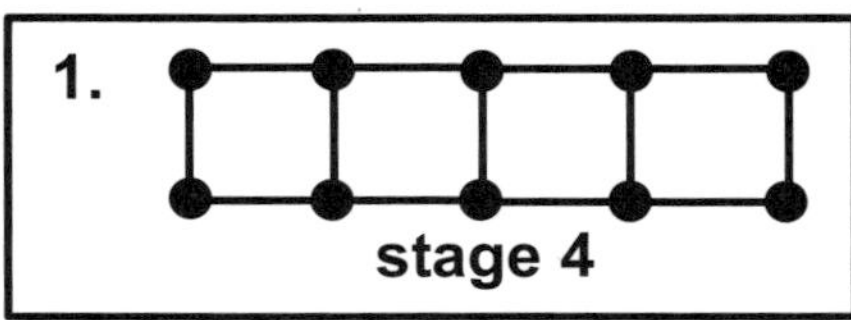

stage 4

2. Stage 4 has 13 toothpicks.

3. Stage 4 has 10 gumdrops.

4. Stage 5 has:

- **16 toothpicks**
- **12 gumdrops**

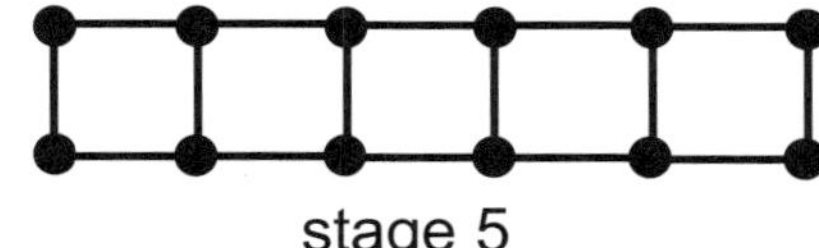

stage 5

5.

stage	1	2	3	4	5	6	7
number of toothpicks	**4**	7	**10**	**13**	**16**	**19**	**22**
number of gumdrops	**4**	6	**8**	**10**	**12**	**14**	**16**

When you increase the stage number by 1, the number of toothpicks goes up by 3 and the number of gumdrops goes up by 2. Continue the pattern to find stage 9.

6. Stage 9 has:

- **28 toothpicks**
- **20 gumdrops**

stage	7	8	9
number of toothpicks	22	25	28
number of gumdrops	16	18	20

7.

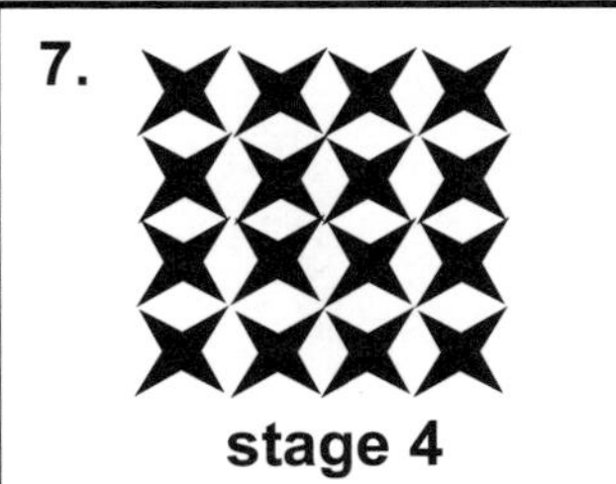

stage 4

8. Stage 4 has 16 stars.

Stage 4 has 4 rows, each with 4 stars, for a total of 4 x 4 = 16 stars.

9. Stage 5 has 25 stars.

Stage 5 has 5 rows, each with 5 stars, for a total of 5 x 5 = 25 stars.

stage 5

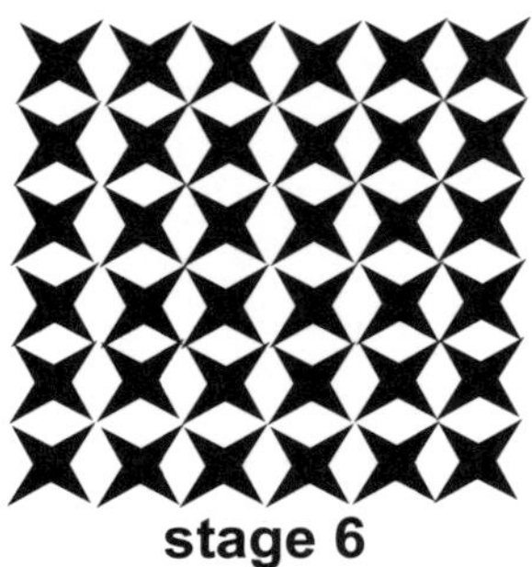
stage 6

10. Stage 6 has 36 stars.

Stage 6 has 6 rows, each with 6 stars, for a total of 6 x 6 = 36 stars.

11. Stage 7 has 49 stars.

Stage 7 has 7 rows, each with 7 stars, for a total of 7 x 7 = 49 stars.

stage 7

12. Stage 10 has 100 stars.

Stage 10 has 10 rows, each with 10 stars, for a total of 10 x 10 = 100 stars.

22. Equality Explorer 5 (p. 27)

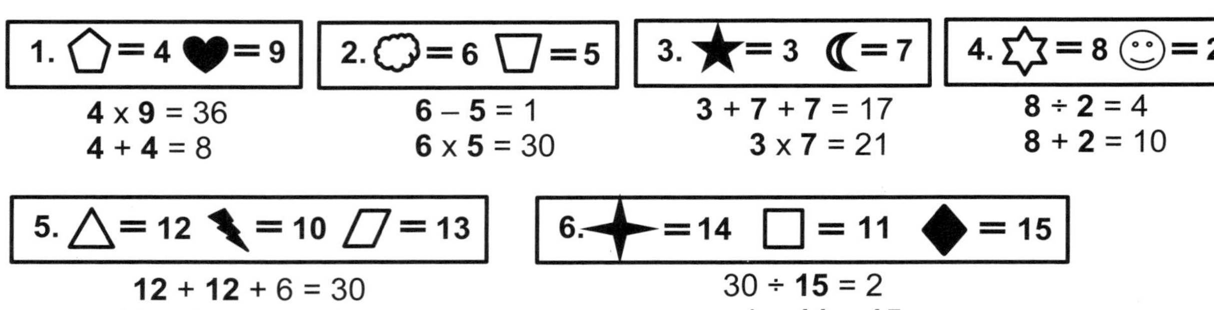

23. Sequence Sleuth 5 (p. 28)

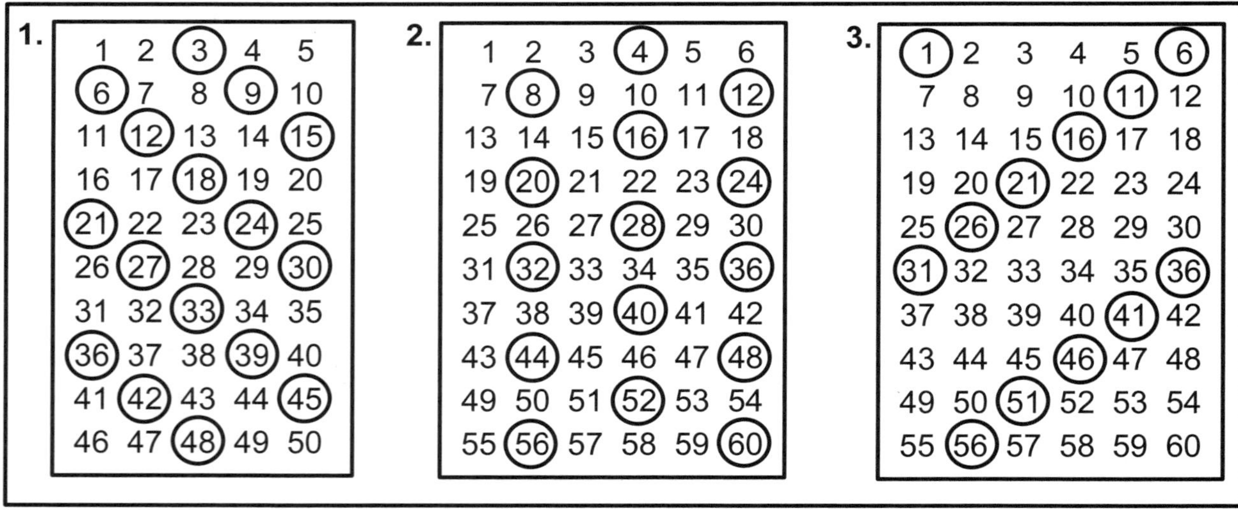

Circled numbers are shown in parentheses.

4.

(1)	2	(3)	4	(5)
6	(7)	8	(9)	10
(11)	12	(13)	14	(15)
16	(17)	18	(19)	20
(21)	22	(23)	24	(25)
26	(27)	28	(29)	30
(31)	32	(33)	34	(35)
36	(37)	38	(39)	40
(41)	42	(43)	44	(45)
46	(47)	48	(49)	50

5.

1	2	(3)	4	5	6
7	8	9	(10)	11	12
13	14	15	16	(17)	18
19	20	21	22	23	(24)
25	26	27	28	29	30
(31)	32	33	34	35	36
37	(38)	39	40	41	42
43	44	(45)	46	47	48
49	50	51	(52)	53	54
55	56	57	58	(59)	60

6.

1	(2)	3	4	5
(6)	7	8	9	(10)
11	12	13	(14)	15
16	17	(18)	19	20
21	(22)	23	24	25
(26)	27	28	29	(30)
31	32	33	(34)	35
36	37	(38)	39	40
41	(42)	43	44	45
(46)	47	48	49	(50)

7. Circled numbers: 3, 9, 15, 21, 27, 33, 39, 45, 51, 57, 63, 69, 75

8. Circled numbers: 3, 6, 9, 12, 15, 18, 21, 24, 27, 30, 33, 36, 39, 42, 45, 48, 51, 54, 57, 60, 63, 66, 69, 72, 75, 78, 81, 84, 87, 90, 93, 96, 99

24. Number Ninja 5 (p. 29)

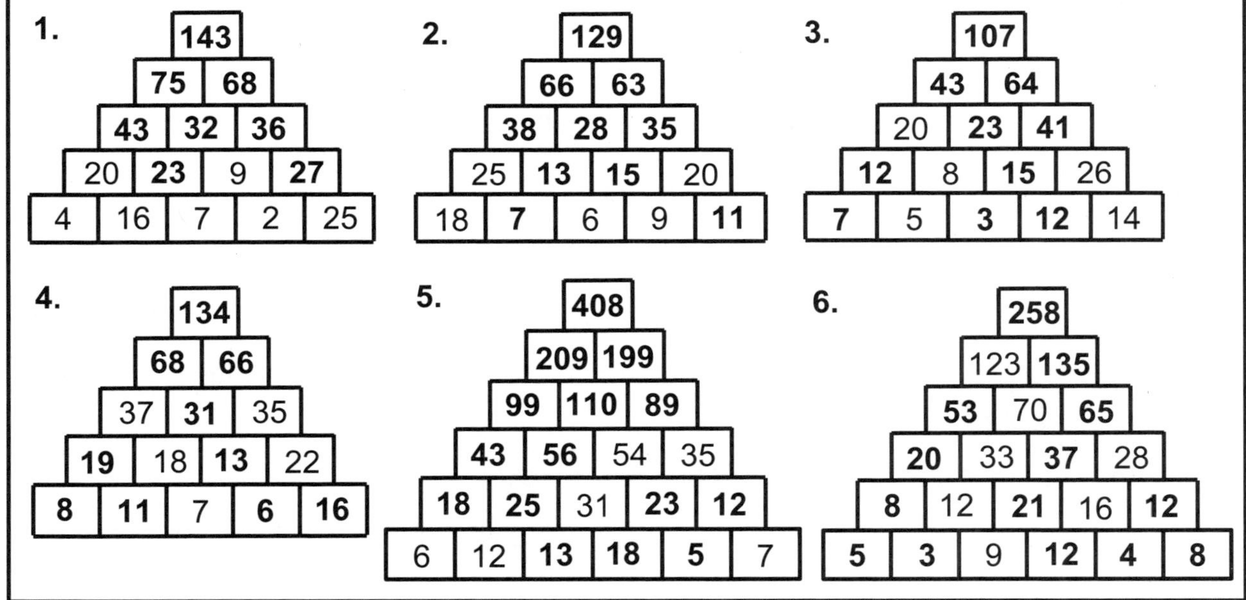

25. Function Finder 5 (p. 30)

1.

in	2	5	7	11	**20**	30
out	14	35	49	**77**	140	**210**

2a. RULE: **multiply by 5**

in	2	6	9	13	**20**	32
out	10	30	45	**65**	100	**160**

2b. RULE: **multiply by 3**

in	2	5	8	12	**16**	22
out	6	15	24	**36**	48	**66**

3a.

gallons	3	5	9	12	**20**	25
quarts	12	20	36	**48**	80	**100**

You multiply the number of gallons by 4 to get the number of quarts:
3 gallons equals 3 x 4 = 12 quarts,
5 gallons equals 5 x 4 = 20 quarts,
9 gallons equals 9 x 4 = 36 quarts, and on.

3b. 60 quarts From 3a, 15 gallons equals 15 x 4 = 60 quarts.

3c. 10 gallons From 3a, 10 gallons equals 10 x 4 = 40 quarts.

4a.

feet	2	3	5	7	**10**	15
inches	24	36	60	**84**	120	**180**

You multiply the number of feet by 12 to get the number of inches:
2 feet equals 2 x 12 = 24 inches,
3 feet equals 3 x 12 = 36 inches,
5 feet equals 5 x 12 = 60 inches, and so on.

4b. 48 inches From 4a, 4 feet equals 4 x 12 = 48 inches.

4c. 6 feet From 4a, 6 feet equals 6 x 12 = 72 inches.

5a.

tickets	1	2	5	8	11	**15**	18
cost ($)	6	12	30	48	**66**	90	**108**

You multiply the number of tickets by 6 to get the cost in dollars:
1 ticket costs 1 x 6 = 6 dollars,
2 tickets cost 2 x 6 = 12 dollars,
5 tickets cost 5 x 6 = 30 dollars, and so on.

5b. 54 dollars From 5a, 9 tickets cost 9 x 6 = 54 dollars.

5c. 7 tickets From 5a, 7 tickets cost 7 x 6 = 42 dollars.

26. Pattern Predictor 6 (p. 31)

1.
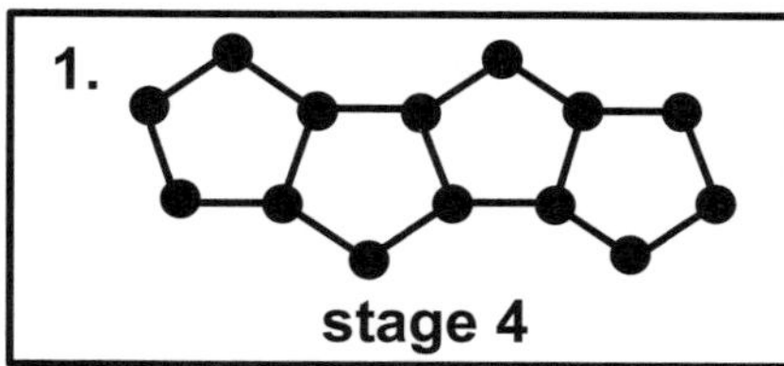
stage 4

2. Stage 4 has 17 toothpicks.

3. Stage 4 has 14 gumdrops.

4. Stage 5 has:

- **21 toothpicks**
- **17 gumdrops**

stage 5

5.

stage	1	2	3	4	5	6	7
number of toothpicks	**5**	9	**13**	**17**	**21**	**25**	**29**
number of gumdrops	**5**	8	**11**	**14**	**17**	**20**	**23**

When you increase the stage number by 1, the number of toothpicks goes up by 4 and the number of gumdrops goes up by 3. Continue the pattern to find stage 10.

6. Stage 10 has:

- **41 toothpicks**
- **32 gumdrops**

stage	7	8	9	10
number of toothpicks	29	33	37	41
number of gumdrops	23	26	29	32

7.

stage 5

8. Stage 5 has 35 circles.

Stage 5 has 7 rows, each with 5 circles, for a total of 7 x 5 = 35 circles.

9. Stage 6 has 48 circles.

Stage 6 has 8 rows, each with 6 circles, for a total of 8 x 6 = 48 circles.

stage 6

10. Stage 7 has 63 circles.

Stage 7 has 9 rows, each with 7 circles, for a total of 9 x 7 = 63 circles.

11. Stage 8 has 80 circles.

Stage 8 has 10 rows, each with 8 circles, for a total of 10 x 8 = 80 circles.

12. Stage 11 has 143 circles.

Stage 11 has 13 rows, each with 11 circles, for a total of 13 x 11 = 143 circles.

27. Equality Explorer 6 (p. 33)

1.

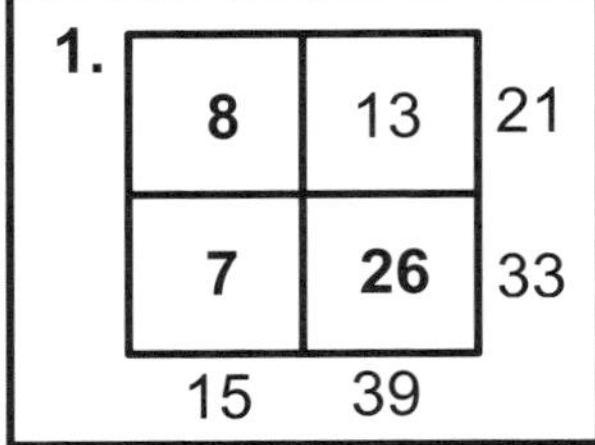

8	13	21
7	**26**	33
15	39	

top row: 8 + 13 = 21
bottom row: 7 + 26 = 33
left column: 8 + 7 = 15
right column: 13 + 26 = 39

2.

3	**21**	5	29
9	**10**	**12**	31
21	17	**6**	44
33	48	23	

top row: 3 + 21 + 5 = 29
middle row: 9 + 10 + 12 = 31
bottom row: 21 + 17 + 6 = 44
left column: 3 + 9 + 21 = 33
middle column: 21 + 10 + 17 = 48
right column: 5 + 12 + 6 = 23

3.

10	7	19	11	47
13	**16**	**2**	4	35
8	**5**	18	25	56
6	9	**3**	**15**	33
37	37	42	55	

4.

13	**20**	16	6	55
3	**12**	15	**8**	38
14	2	9	4	29
7	**5**	**23**	10	45
37	39	63	28	

28. Sequence Sleuth 6 (p. 34)

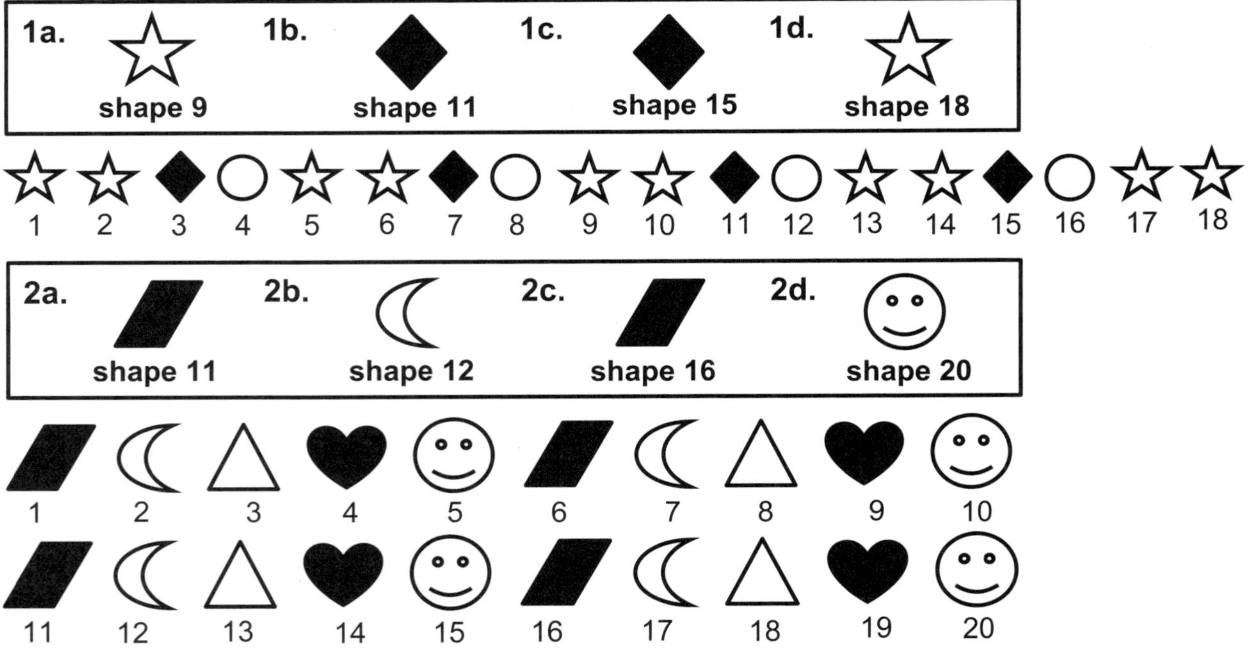

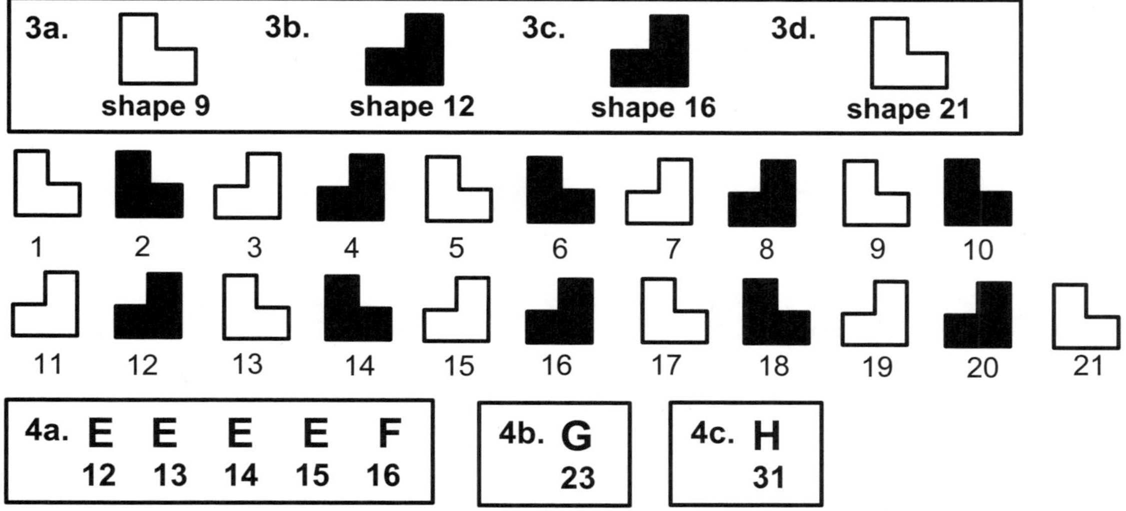

The sequence has 1 A, then 2 Bs, then 3 Cs, then 4 Ds, then 5 Es, then 6 Fs, then 7 Gs, then 8 Hs, and so on.

A	B	B	C	C	C	D	D	D	D	E	E	E	E	E	F
1	2	3	4	5	6	7	8	9	10	11	12	13	14	15	16

F	F	F	F	F	G	G	G	G	G	G	G	H	H	H
17	18	19	20	21	22	23	24	25	26	27	28	29	30	31

29. Number Ninja 6 (p. 35)

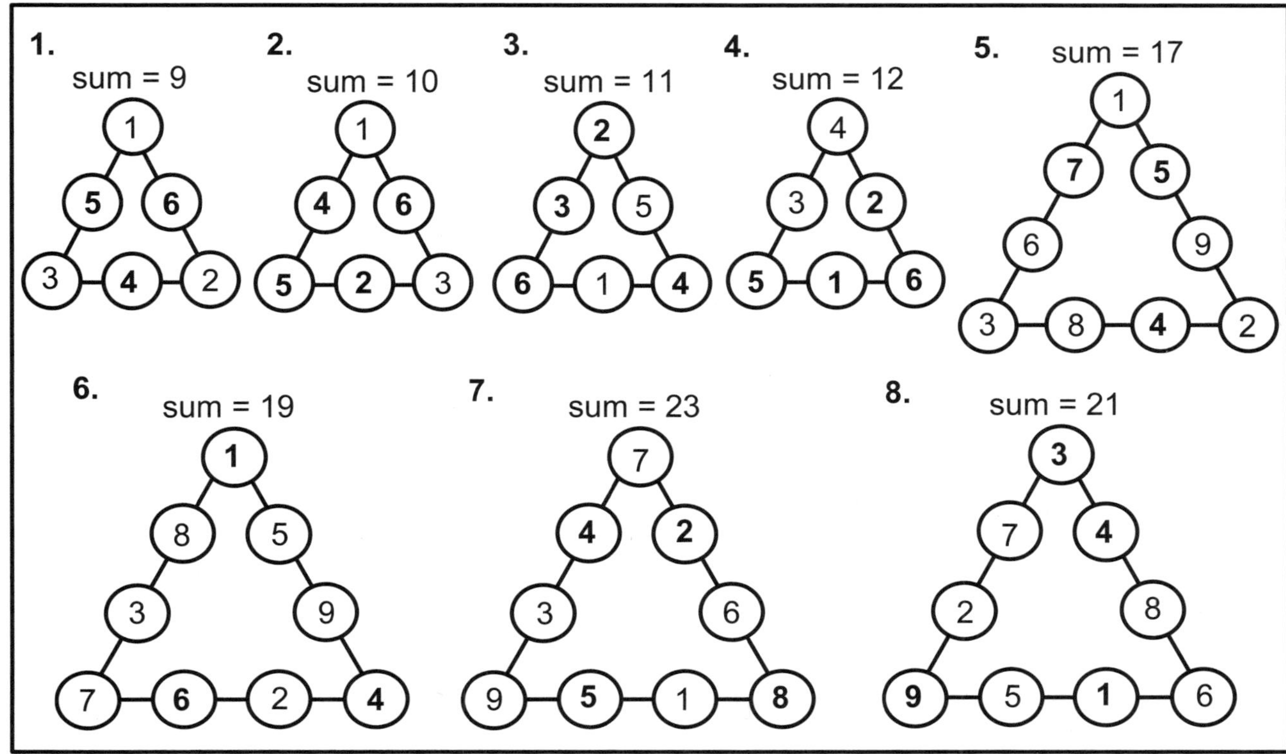

30. Function Finder 6 (p. 36)

1.

in	4	9	16	21	**32**	54
out	17	22	29	**34**	45	**67**

2a. RULE: **add 10**

in	14	21	29	36	**42**	74
out	24	31	39	**46**	52	**84**

2b. RULE: **add 22**

in	6	13	18	25	**42**	57
out	28	35	40	**47**	64	**79**

3a.

Spencer's age	5	11	23	35	**44**	66
Amanda's age	13	19	31	**43**	52	**74**

Amanda is 8 years older than Spencer: when Spencer is 5, Amanda is 13, when Spencer is 11, Amanda is 19, and on.

3b. Amanda is 24. Amanda is 8 years older than Spencer: 8 + 16 = 24.

3c. Spencer is 39. Spencer is 8 years younger than Amanda: 47 – 8 = 39.

4a.

cost to make cake ($)	6	9	15	22	28	**36**
selling price of cake ($)	11	14	20	27	**33**	41

The cake's selling price is $5 more than the cost to make the cake.

4b. The cake's selling price is $30. The cake's selling price is $5 more than the $25 cost to make the cake: $5 + $25 = $30.

4c. The cost to make the cake is $12. The cost to make the cake is $5 less than the $17 selling price of cake: $17 – $5 = $12.

5a.

Sammy's situps	20	32	45	57	70	**103**
Sammy's pushups	5	17	30	42	**55**	88

Each day Sammy does 15 less pushups than situps.

5b. Sammy does 12 pushups. Sammy does 15 less pushups than his 27 situps: 27 – 15 = 12.

5c. Sammy does 65 situps. Sammy does 15 more situps than his 50 pushups: 50 + 15 = 65.

31. Pattern Predictor 7 (p. 37)

1.

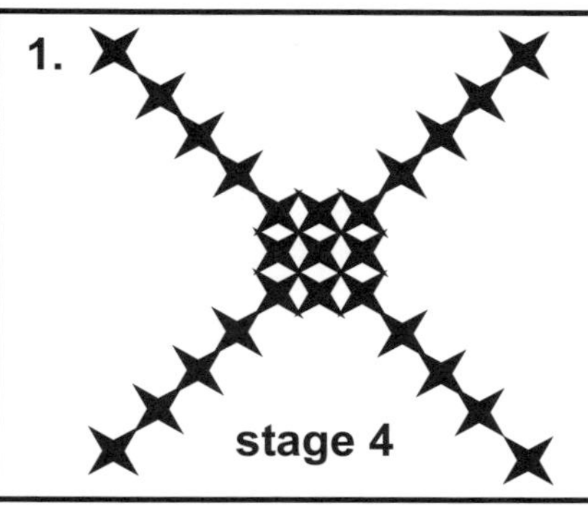

2. Stage 4 has 25 stars.

Stage 4 has 4 branches, each with 4 stars, plus 9 stars in the middle for a total of 4 x 4 + 9 = 16 + 9 = 25 stars.

3. Stage 5 has 29 stars.

Stage 5 has 4 branches, each with 5 stars, plus 9 stars in the middle for a total of 4 x 5 + 9 = 20 + 9 = 29 stars.

4.

stage	1	2	3	4	5	6	7
number of stars	13	**17**	**21**	**25**	**29**	**33**	**37**

5. Stage 8 has 41 stars.

Stage 8 has 4 branches, each with 8 stars, plus 9 stars in the middle for a total of 4 x 8 + 9 = 32 + 9 = 41 stars.

6. Stage 12 has 57 stars.

Stage 12 has 4 branches, each with 12 stars, plus 9 stars in the middle for a total of 4 x 12 + 9 = 48 + 9 = 57 stars.

A more complete table helps you understand the answers to questions 5 and 6.

stage	1	2	3	4	5	6	7	8	9	10	11	12
number of stars	13	**17**	**21**	**25**	**29**	**33**	**37**	**41**	**45**	**49**	**53**	**57**

7.

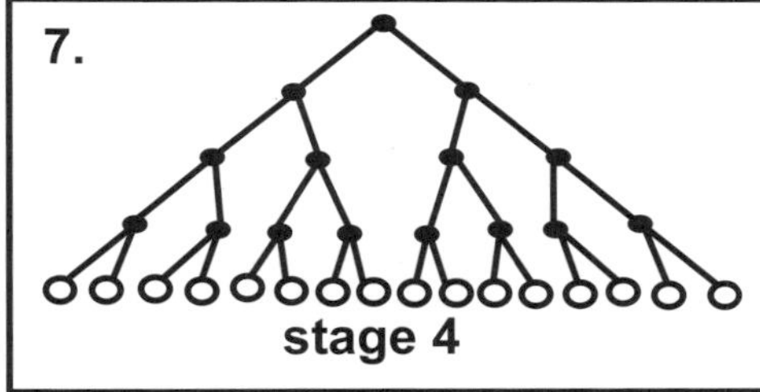

8.

stage	number of open dots
1	2
2	4
3	8
4	16

9. When you increase the stage number by 1, the number of open dots doubles.

- **stage 5 has 32 open dots**
- **stage 6 has 64 open dots**

10. Stage 8 has 256 open dots.

Follow the pattern and keep doubling: stage 6 has 64 open dots, stage 7 has 128 open dots, stage 8 has 256 open dots.

32. Equality Explorer 7 (p. 39)

1. ◇ = 5 ☾ = 13

5 x **5** = 25
5 + **5** + **5** = **13** + 2

2. ⬠ = 2 ⚡ = 3

2 x **2** x **2** = 8
2 x **3** x **3** = 18

3. ☺ = 6 ♡ = 10

6 + **3** = 9
10 + **10** + **5** = 25

Note: ◐ = 3 (half ♡) = 5

4. ✡ = 9 ▰ = 1

9 + **1** = 10
9 – **1** = 8

5. ▲ = 4 ☁ = 8 □ = 12

8 x **4** = 32
8 ÷ **4** = 2
4 + **12** = 16

6. ⏢ = 11 ✦ = 15 ○ = 7

11 + **11** – 7 = **15**
15 ÷ 3 = 5
3 + **15** – **11** = **7**

33. Sequence Sleuth 7 (p. 40)

1. A: 91, 85, 79, 73, 67, 61, 55, 49
B: 59, 53, 47, **41**, 35, 29, **23**, 17
C: 64, 58, 52, 46, **40**, **34**, 28, **22**
D: 80, 74, **68**, **62**, 56, 50, **44**, **38**

Subtract 6 to go from one term to the next.

2. A: 5, 6, 8, 11, 15, 20, 26, 33
B: 22, 23, 25, 28, 32, 37, **43**, 50
C: 67, 68, 70, 73, **77**, 82, **88**, 95
D: 39, 40, **42**, 45, **49**, 54, **60**, 67

Add 1, then add 2, then add 3, then add 4, then add 5, and so on.

3. A: 11, 15, 16, 20, 21, 25, 26, 30
B: 18, 22, 23, 27, 28, 32, **33**, 37
C: 46, 50, 51, 55, **56**, 60, **61**, **65**
D: 77, 81, **82**, 86, **87**, **91**, 92, **96**

Add 4, then add 1, then add 4, then add 1, and so on.

4. A: 70, 62, 60, 52, 50, 42, 40, 32
B: 85, 77, 75, 67, **65**, 57, 55, **47**
C: 94, 86, 84, 76, **74**, **66**, 64, **56**
D: 89, 81, 79, **71**, **69**, 61, **59**, **51**

Subtract 8, then subtract 2, then subtract 8, then subtract 2, and so on.

5. A: 5, 10, 20, 40, 80, 160
B: 2, 4, 8, 16, **32**, **64**
C: 3, 6, 12, **24**, 48, **96**
D: 7, 14, 28, **56**,112, **224**

Multiply by 2 to go from one term to the next.

6. A: 40, 32, 35, 27, 30, 22, 25, 17
B: 58, 50, 53, 45, 48, 40, **43**, **35**
C: 94, 86, 89, 81, **84**, 76, **79**, **71**
D: 73, 65, 68, **60**, **63**, 55, **58**, **50**

Subtract 8, then add 3, then subtract 8, then add 3, and so on.

34. Number Ninja 7 (p. 41)

1. 27 + **36 =** 9 x 7
27 + **36 =** 63

2. 48 – **33 =** 60 ÷ 4
48 – **33** = 15

3. 83 – 38 **=** 3 x **15**
45 **=** 3 x **15**

4. 36 ÷ **9 =** 19 – 15
36 ÷ **9 =** 4

5. 34 + 18 **=** 19 + **10** + 23
52 **=** 19 + **10** + 23

6. 21 + 17 – **26 =** 48 ÷ 4
38 – **26 =** 12

7. **68** ÷ 17 = 32 ÷ 8
68 ÷ 17 **=** 4

8. 8 x 9 **= 12** x 6
72 = **12** x 6

9. 60 – **21** = 11 + 13 + 15
60 – **21 =** 39

10. 77 + **9** = 104 – 18
77 + **9 =** 86

11. **2** x **4** + **8** = 16 **or**
4 x **2** + **8** = 16
8 + 8 = 16

12. **6** + **8** – **2** = 12 **or**
8 + **6** – **2** = 12
14 – 2 **=** 12

13. **4** x **8** – **2** = 30 **or**
8 x **4** – **2** = 30
32 – 2 **=** 30

14. **8** ÷ **4** + **2** = 4
2 + 2 = 4

15. **4** + **6** – **2** = 8 **or**
6 + **4** – **2** = 8
10 – 2 **=** 8

16. **2** x **8** + **6** = 22 **or**
8 x **2** + **6** = 22
16 + 6 = 22

17. **2** x **4** x **8** = 64 **or**
any order of 2, 4, 8
8 x 8 = 64

18. **2** + **4** + **8** = 14 **or**
any order of 2, 4, 8
6 + 8 **=** 14

35. Function Finder 7 (p. 42)

1a.

# of cheeseburgers	3	5	8	10	14	**18**	20
total cost ($)	15	25	40	50	**70**	90	100

Each cheeseburger costs $5. 3 cheeseburgers cost $15, 5 cheeseburgers cost $25, and so on.

1b. The total cost of 30 cheeseburgers is $150.

Each cheeseburger costs $5, so the total cost of 30 cheeseburgers is 30 x $5 = $150.

1c. 12 cheeseburgers have a total cost of $60.

Each cheeseburger costs $5, so the total cost of 12 cheeseburgers is 12 x $5 = $60.

2a.

start	8:00 am	9:15 am	10:20 am	1:30 pm	3:25 pm	**4:40 pm**	8:05 pm
end	8:40 am	9:55 am	11:00 am	2:10 pm	**4:05 pm**	5:20 pm	8:45 pm

Each class is 40 minutes long.

2b. The class ends at 12:25 pm.

The class ends 40 minutes after the 11:45 am start, which is 12:25 pm.

2c. The class starts at 2:30 pm.

The class starts 40 minutes before the 3:10 pm ending, which is 2:30 pm.

3a.

minutes walking	1	5	8	20	30	**40**	50
calories burned	4	20	32	80	**120**	160	200

Each minute of walking burns 4 calories: 5 minutes burns 20 calories, 8 minutes burns 32 calories, and so on.

3b. 25 minutes of walking burns 100 calories.

Each minute of walking burns 4 calories, so 25 minutes of walking burns 25 x 4 calories = 100 calories.

3c. 12 minutes of walking are needed to burn 48 calories.

Each minute of walking burns 4 calories, so 12 minutes of walking burns 12 x 4 calories = 48 calories.

4a.

teacher's age	28	35	42	50	57	**62**	68
years teaching	6	13	20	28	**35**	40	46

The number of years teaching is 22 years less than the teacher's age.

4b. At the age of 45, the teacher has taught 23 years.

At the age of 45, the teacher has taught 45 – 22 = 23 years.

4c. When the teacher has taught 9 years, she is 31 years old.

When she has taught 9 years, her age is 9 + 22 = 31.

36. Pattern Predictor 8 (p. 43)

1. Stage 5 has 26 hearts.

Stage 5 has 6 + 4 + 6 + 4 + 6 = 26 hearts.

stage 5

2. Stage 6 has 30 hearts.

Stage 6 has 6 + 4 + 6 + 4 + 6 + 4= 30 hearts.

stage 6

3.

stage	1	2	3	4	5	6	7	8
number of hearts	**6**	**10**	**16**	**20**	**26**	**30**	**36**	**40**

4. Stage 11 has 56 hearts.

5. Stage 14 has 70 hearts.

A more complete table helps you understand the answers to questions 4 and 5.

stage	1	2	3	4	5	6	7	8	9	10	11	12	13	14
number of hearts	6	10	16	20	26	30	36	40	46	50	56	60	66	70

6. 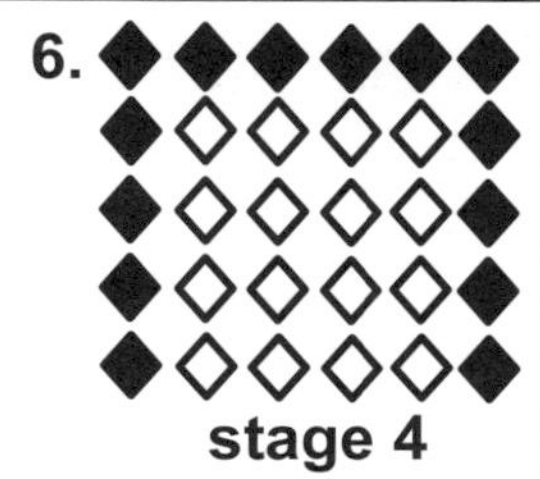

stage 4

7. Stage 4 has 16 unshaded diamonds.

8. Stage 4 has 14 shaded diamonds.

9. Stage 5 has:
- **25 unshaded diamonds**
- **17 shaded diamonds**
- **42 diamonds in total**

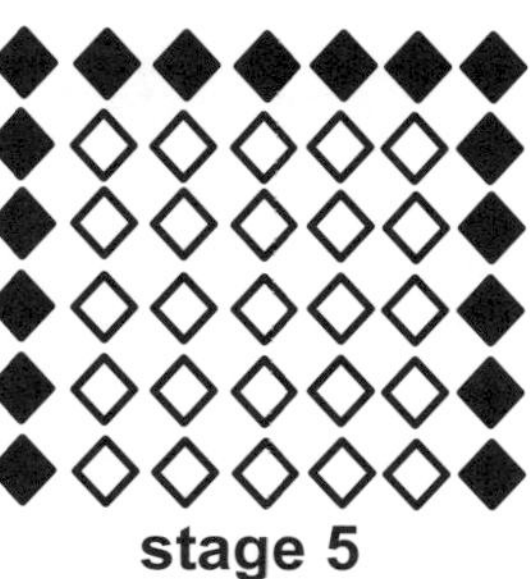

stage 5

10.

stage	1	2	3	4	5	6	7
number of unshaded diamonds	1	**4**	**9**	**16**	**25**	**36**	**49**
number of shaded diamonds	5	**8**	**11**	**14**	**17**	**20**	**23**
total number of diamonds	6	**12**	**20**	**30**	**42**	**56**	**72**

11. Stage 10 has:
- **100 unshaded diamonds**
- **32 shaded diamonds**
- **132 diamonds in total**

Continuing the patterns helps you understand the answer to question 11.

stage	7	8	9	10
number of unshaded diamonds	49	64	81	100
number of shaded diamonds	23	26	29	32
total number of diamonds	72	90	110	132

37. Equality Explorer 8 (p. 45)

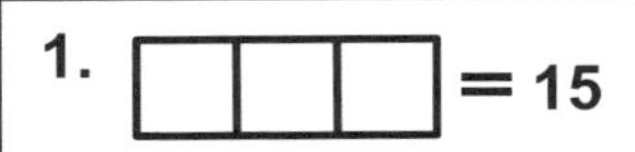

1 square is worth 5, so 3 squares are worth 15.

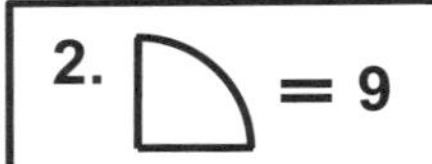

A full circle is worth 36, so a quarter circle is worth 36 ÷ 4 = 9.

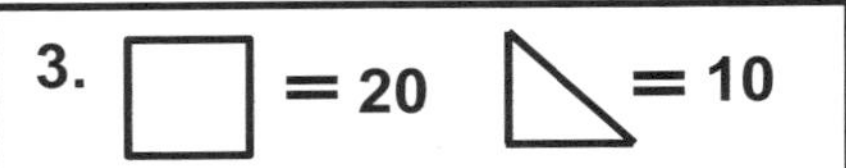

2 squares are worth 40, so 1 square is worth 20 and half a square (a triangle) is worth 10.

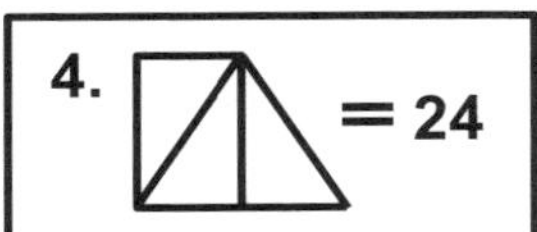

The rectangle is worth 16, so half a rectangle (a triangle) is worth 8 and 3 triangles are worth 24.

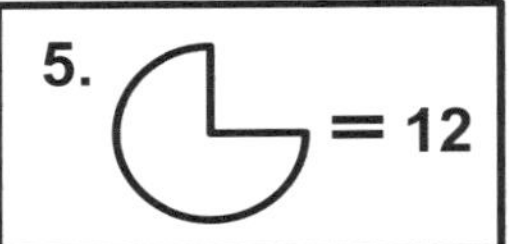

A full circle is worth 16, so a quarter circle is worth 16 ÷ 4 = 4. Three-quarters of a circle is worth 3 x 4 = 12.

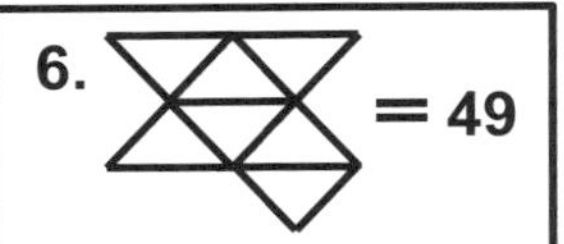

3 triangles are worth 21, so 1 triangle is worth 7. Seven triangles are worth 7 x 7 = 49.

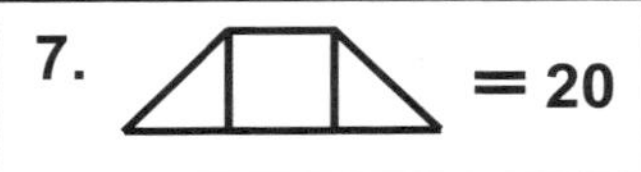

A square plus a half-square (a triangle) is worth 15, so the square is worth 10 and the triangle is worth 5. The square plus 2 triangles are worth 10 + 5 + 5 = 20.

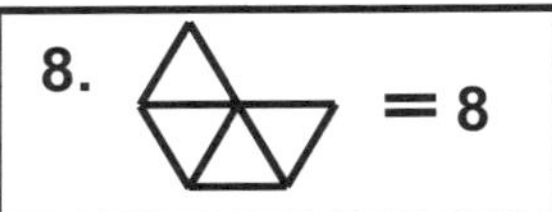

Six triangles are worth 12, so 1 triangle is worth 2. Four triangles are worth 4 x 2 = 8.

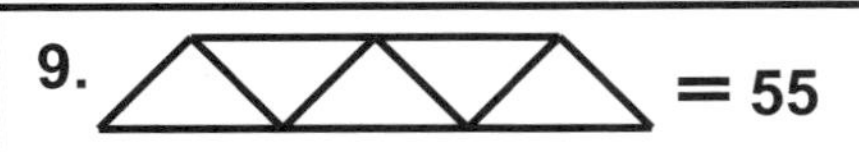

Two triangles are worth 22, so 1 triangle is worth 11. Five triangles are worth 5 x 11 = 55.

10. = 3

Four squares are worth 24, so 1 square is worth 6 and a half-square (a triangle) is worth 3.

38. Sequence Sleuth 8 (p. 46)

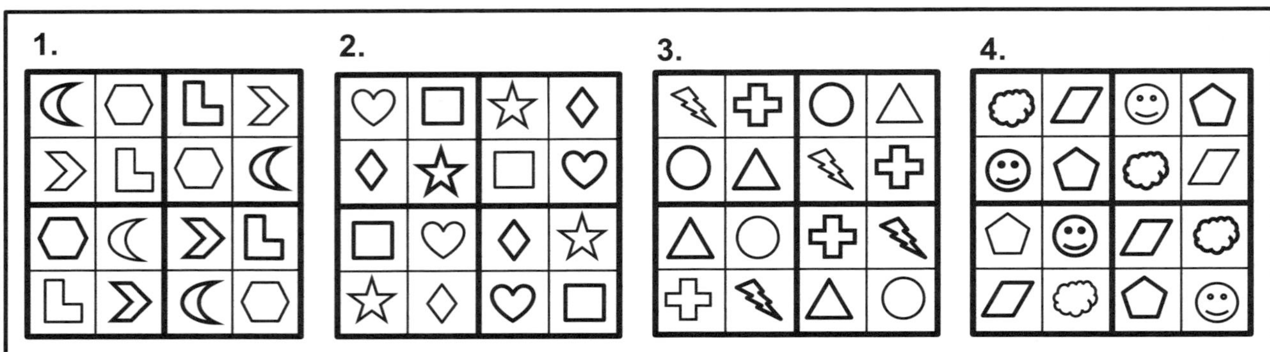

39. Number Ninja 8 (p. 47)

1. $27 + 56 = 83$
2. $43 - 18 = 25$
3. $26 \times 3 = 78$
4. $62 + 38 = 100$
5. $328 - 53 = 275$
6. $243 + 697 = 940$
7. $37 \times 4 = 148$
8. $565 + 387 = 952$
9. $894 - 346 = 548$
10. $283 \times 4 = 1132$
11. $928 + 769 = 1697$
12. $342 - 287 = 55$

40. Function Finder 8 (p. 48)

1. RULE: ***ADD 4***

in	6	17	30	53	75	***92***	100
out	10	21	34	57	***79***	96	104

2. RULE: ***MULTIPLY BY 2***

in	1	5	12	25	30	***44***	133
out	2	10	24	50	***60***	88	266

3. RULE: **multiply by 3**

in	2	5	8	11	20	**40**	100
out	6	15	24	33	**60**	120	300

4. RULE: **add 11**

in	25	40	88	100	143	**204**	270
out	36	51	99	111	**154**	215	281

5. RULE: **subtract 7**

in	30	48	67	100	149	**181**	207
out	23	41	60	93	**142**	174	200

6. RULE: **divide by 5**

in	5	15	40	100	250	**300**	500
out	1	3	8	20	**50**	60	100

7. RULE: **add 3**

in	30	42	67	81	93	**108**	97
out	33	45	70	84	**96**	111	100

8. RULE: **multiply by 10**

in	1	4	7	12	19	**28**	49
out	10	40	70	120	**190**	280	490

9. RULE: **divide by 2**

in	6	22	40	66	84	**92**	100
out	3	11	20	33	**42**	46	50

10. RULE: **subtract 5**

in	16	27	59	90	148	**211**	395
out	11	22	54	85	**143**	206	390

Dare to Compare Math Level 1 Sample

25. Who travels the longest distance? Who travels the shortest distance?

Tanya walks 4 feet every second for 60 seconds.

Kevin cycles 30 feet every second for 7 seconds.

Amanda runs 9 feet every second for 25 seconds.

26. Joanne and Remy each build a wooden fence around their rectangular vegetable garden. Whose fence costs more?

Joanne's fence costs $7 per meter.

15 m

10 m 10 m

15 m

Remy's fence costs $5 per meter.

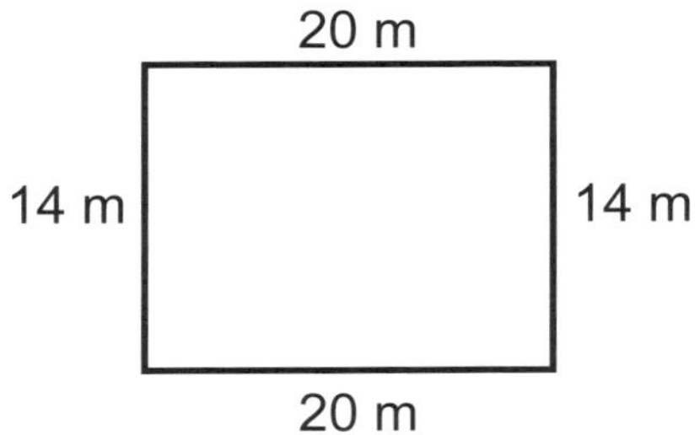

27. In the list below, each person's heart beats at a constant rate. Whose heart will have the most beats in 1 minute? Whose heart will have the fewest beats in 1 minute?

- Adam's heart beats 25 times in 20 seconds.
- Rachel's heart beats 160 times in 120 seconds.
- Brett's heart beats 18 times in 15 seconds.